Malachi

BOOKS IN THE BIBLE STUDY COMMENTARY SERIES

*Not yet published as of this printing.

BIBLE STUDY COMMENTARY

Malachi

CHARLES D. ISBELL

Lamplighter Books Grand Rapids, Michigan
Zondervan Publishing House

MALACHI: A STUDY GUIDE COMMENTARY
© 1980 by The Zondervan Corporation
Grand Rapids, Michigan

Lamplighter Books are published by Zondervan
Publishing House, 1415 Lake Drive, S.E.,
Grand Rapids, Michigan 49506

Library of Congress Cataloging in Publication Data
Isbell, Charles D
    Malachi: a commentary study guide.

    Bibliography: p.
    1. Bible. O.T. Malachi—Commentaries. I. Title.
BS1675.3.I8   224'.9907   80-14130
ISBN 0-310-41673-6 (pbk.)

Edited by Arnold Jantzen and Gerard Terpstra

Printed in the United States of America

88   89   90   91   92   93   94 / EP / 10   9   8   7   6   5   4

Contents

Chapter 1

Introduction

A. Significance of the Book of Malachi

The Book of Malachi closes the English Old Testament and marks the end of the prophetic section of the Hebrew Scriptures. This book has long played a significant role both in Jewish and in Christian tradition, not only because of its physical presence in the Bible but also because of the various ways in which it has lent itself to fruitful interpretation.

Jews recognize the tradition contained in their Babylonian Talmud that teaches that with the death of Haggai, Zechariah, and Malachi (the latest prophets in the traditional view) the Holy Spirit departed from Israel. Following this departure of the Holy Spirit, it became necessary for God to communicate with the people of Israel in a nonimmediate way. This tradition points to, among other things, Malachi's significance as the very last of those prophets who had communicated with Israel *directly* from God.

In Christian tradition the Book of Malachi is important both because of its place in the Old Testament and because of several uses that the New Testament authors made of the book. In Mark 1:2–4 the messianic herald mentioned in Malachi 3:1 is equated with John the Baptist, who prepared the way for the coming of Jesus the Messiah. And Jesus Himself understood that John was the fulfillment of Malachi's vision of Elijah as the forerunner of the Lord, who was coming to His people (compare Malachi 4:5–6 with Mark 9:11–13 and Luke 1:13, 16–17).

B. Name and Title of the Book

The Hebrew word rendered in English as "Malachi" is not a proper name. It is, rather, a common noun, translated "my messenger" (cf.

Mal. 3:1). "Malachi" is composed of two elements— the noun *mal'akh* ("messenger") and the suffix pronoun *y* ("my"), 'which is the letter *i* in English. For this reason it is commonly agreed that the author of the messages that comprise the bulk of the Book of Malachi was not named by the editor of the book (see below). This makes the book one of several anonymous portions of literature that have come to be part of our sacred Scriptures. Lacking the name of the original preacher of these messages, the biblical editor evidently chose the word *Malachi* to function as the title of the work. This choice, as we shall see, also served to identify the book with one of its major ideas, as expressed in the opening verses of the third chapter.

C. Date of the Book

The date of Malachi, at least within broad boundaries, is clear from several internal clues. Because the temple in Jerusalem was being used for religious ceremony and worship, the book must have been composed in its present form at least sometime later than 516 B.C., when the temple rebuilding project was completed. On the other hand, there is in Malachi no apparent awareness of official legislation against mixed marriages. This probably means that the book in its present form precedes the year 444 B.C., when there were instituted in Jerusalem precisely such specific marital rules.

At some point between these two dates (516 and 444 B.C.) Malachi can be viewed as the prophetic voice decrying many of the ills that the blunt measures of Ezra and Nehemiah were soon to address from a priestly viewpoint and a political one respectively (see F. below).

A final piece of evidence commonly used to help set a date for the composition of the Book of Malachi is the use of the word *pehah* in 1:8. *Pehah* is a Persian word meaning "governor," and its presence in the text points to a time broadly within the era of Persian domination in the ancient Near East (c. 536 to 332 B.C.).

On the basis of these few internal clues, precise dating of Malachi is impossible. However, it can be noted that there is rather widespread scholarly agreement for dating the book at approximately 460 or 450 B.C.

D. Literary Style of the Book

This anonymous piece of prophecy to which a title has been added as described above is, despite all lack of knowledge relating to authorship, a superb example of the style of argumentation that came to be widely practiced in Jewish literature in the fifth century B.C. and subsequent periods. This style was characterized by three basic elements. First, a very strong, almost shocking, statement was made in the form of a frontal attack on the audience or the readers. In this shocking statement was presented a general truth that the speaker-author intended to defend. But the style was so obviously abrasive that a negative reaction against it was to be expected on all sides.

Second, the speaker or the author attempted to anticipate the major question or objection that the abrasive opening declaration had caused in the minds of the hearers or the readers. On the basis of this anticipation he himself then posed the question that he believed the readers or audience would raise. However, though the question or objection was actually raised by the *author*, it was attributed to the *audience!* In this way it appeared that a dialogue was developing between the speaker and the audience, when in actual fact only one speaker was involved, and he alone was responsible for both points of view. A single example will illustrate the point here. In chapter 1:7 the priests are quoted as having said, "The Lord's table is contemptible." Now no one should suppose that any priest would have actually dared to have said precisely that. What is meant in the verse is rather that the *actions* of the priests (described in vv. 8 and 13) indicated their true feelings, no matter what they did or did not say aloud. By their sloppy handling of sacred duties, they were testifying to their actual thinking about the business of serving God. As we might say it, their actions spoke louder than their words. So the prophet very bluntly put into words the implications of their actions, and thereby he set the stage for the rebuke that he later delivered to the priests for their inferior performances.

Third, the author or speaker proceeded to elaborate on the original point by using illustrations from history, from earlier biblical materials, or from contemporary events. Also introduced at this juncture were factual data that the author interpreted so as to answer the objection that had been attributed to the audience in the preceding sentence.

This format of strong, abrasive statement; of anticipated objection or question; and of elaboration on the original theme combined with answering of specific objections that could be raised appears clearly throughout the short book. In fact, there are six units in Malachi that fit this general mold (see outline below), although some of the six, as we will observe later, present these three parts rather imprecisely.

E. Structure and Outline of the Book

As indicated above, the structure and outline of the Book of Malachi are quite plain and easy to discover; the chapter divisions of this book will follow the outline of Malachi given below:

    I. The Superscription (1:1)
    II. The Love and the Hatred of God (1:2–5)
    III. The Sins of the Priests (1:6–2:9)
    IV. A Community in Covenant (2:10–16)
    V. The Problem of God's Justice (2:17–3:5)
    VI. The Sins of Lay Persons (3:6–12)
    VII. The Problem of Serving God (3:13–4:3)
    VIII. The Conclusion (4:4–6)

F. The Historical and Theological Setting of the Book

The middle of the fifth century B.C. was a significant period in the development of ancient Israel's theological understanding. From the time of the reign of David over a unified Israel, prophetic support had consistently been given to the doctrine of the eternality of Davidic leadership in Jerusalem. According to this line of reckoning, David and his successors would continue to occupy the throne in Jerusalem no matter what else might be happening in the world. If any of them flagrantly sinned, God would punish them (see esp. 2 Sam. 7:14). But in no case, so it was believed, would the kingship be taken away from the dynasty of David. The classical expression of this doctrine is summarized in 2 Samuel 7:16: "Your house and your kingdom will endure forever before me; your throne will be established forever."

According to the biblical record no prophet questioned the truth of this doctrine for many years. And along with this belief in the eternality of the Davidic dynasty also stood the belief in the indestructibility of Jerusalem, the city of David. These twin pillars, then, constituted a starting point for biblical theologians from the time of David onward. The only exception appears to be a verse in Micah 3:12, where the prophet foresaw the time of Jerusalem's destruction because she, like Samaria before her, had become so wicked that God would be compelled to destroy her to purify her from her sins. This single verse, itself denied to the Micah of the eighth century by many scholars, who assign it to a time after Jeremiah in the late seventh century, represents the only crack in the armor of these twin doctrines: the eternality of David and the indestructibility of Jerusalem (with her temple).

The situation concerning these two beliefs began to change radically with the ministry of Jeremiah. Concerned about the moral decadence widely spread throughout Judean society, Jeremiah recalled another ancient tradition that could be used to challenge overdependency on the idea of maintaining national security through Davidic, dynastic leadership. Accordingly, the question that Jeremiah raised was whether God could continue to defend against all foes a city that was becoming increasingly unworthy of His name. Acquainted with venerable covenantal beliefs that reached all the way back to Mt. Sinai, Jeremiah emphasized the conditional nature of the promises that God had made to His people. Always, Jeremiah understood, the blessing and protection of God were dependent on and related closely to the obedience of His people. This meant, among other things, that the strict social and ethical requirements of Mosaic legislation could not be ignored. No matter what may have been promised to David, and despite the apparently airtight wording of the promise delivered to him by a prophet so honorable as Nathan, the ethical requirements of Yahweh were perceived by Jeremiah to be still in force.

By beginning his theological system with divine standards for ethics, justice, and social morality, Jeremiah reached a conclusion that his fellow countrymen clearly believed to be shocking and dangerous, if not downright blasphemous. If it is true that God demands obedience to His ethical standards, and if Jerusalem should persist in disobeying these standards, only one conclusion was possible. Jerusalem would be treated to the fate that had befallen Shiloh centuries earlier. Shiloh, itself once a religious center in ancient Israel and the scene of annual religious festivals (Judg. 21:19), once also the professional home of the renowned Samuel (see 1 Sam. 1–3), had been destroyed as the religious center of Israel. In comparing Jerusalem to Shiloh, Jeremiah was saying what no one else dared to imagine—Jerusalem *could* fall! If she continued to witness stealing, murdering, adulterous, perjurious, idolatrous folk living within her walls (see Jer. 7:9), even queenly Jerusalem could fall—just as Shiloh did (see Jer. 7:12; 26:6).

The reaction against Jeremiah's preaching was drastic. Religious officials ruled, "This man should be sentenced to death because he has prophesied against this city" (Jer. 26:11). Jeremiah narrowly escaped when the earlier prediction of doom by Micah discussed above was cited to prove that other prophets had been allowed to live even though they had been clearly wrong about Jerusalem (Jer. 26:17–19).

And after suffering years of humiliation and alienation from his own people because of his message (see, e.g., Jer. 20:7–8), Jeremiah was left to die in a muddy cistern (Jer. 38:6). Indeed, but for the kindness of a friend, he would have perished out of sight and out of mind (see Jer. 38:7–14).

Perhaps the hardest thing Jeremiah faced during his career was total alienation from fellow prophets. You see, while Jeremiah was pressing his message on the people of Jerusalem, scores of highly respectable, evidently sincere, and officially ordained men of God were busy saying just the opposite. They preached that Jerusalem simply could not fall because she was, after all, the city of David, who was the chosen one of God. Though Jeremiah argued that they were incorrect and were merely filling the people with ungrounded false hope (Jer. 23:16), even he admitted that their message was what he would like to be able to believe (Jer. 28:6). And, at the time, those who opposed Jeremiah certainly had a great deal of evidence that they could marshal against him. Years earlier, Isaiah had guided Jerusalem through the worst crisis anyone could possibly imagine. Almost two hundred thousand Assyrian troops had laid siege to Jerusalem. Given their experience at conquering fortified cities and their clear superiority to Judah in military matters generally, Jerusalem must surely have appeared to even the most ardent patriot to be doomed. But Isaiah had said:

> He [the king of Assyria] will not enter this city
>   or shoot an arrow here.
> He will not come before it with shield
>   or build a siege ramp against it.
> By the way that he came he will return;
>   he will not enter this city, declares the Lord.
> I will defend this city and save it,
>   for my sake and for the sake of David my servant!
>   (Isa. 37:33–35).

What happened following this prediction? The angel of Yahweh slaughtered 185,000 Assyrian soldiers, scattering dead bodies throughout the camp and forcing the Assyrians to withdraw exactly as Isaiah had said (see Isa. 37:36–37). How about that, Jeremiah? Jerusalem had been sinful then, too, as Isaiah himself had seen clearly (e.g., Isa. 1:21–23; 5:8–25). And Jerusalem had required purging from God in those days, again as Isaiah had realized (e.g., Isa. 1:18; 6:5). But destruction? Impossible. "History proves," Jeremiah's opponents were able to say with great justification and authority, "that Yahweh defends David's city against the worst enemies imaginable."

Yet another aspect of the ministry of Jeremiah led to his undoing. Public officials, bolstered by the more pleasant messages of Jeremiah's fellow professionals, feared that the doctrine of Jeremiah was dangerous. Not because people might believe him (there were too many sermons on "peace" in town to make it likely that large numbers would ever attend Jeremiah's church), but there was a danger far more real. By *saying* such dastardly words of doom, Jeremiah could well be contributing to the possibility of doom (see chapter one and the comments on the word *davar*). So he had to be stopped. It was the necessary thing to do. One prophet must be denied freedom to speak those awful and malicious things so that the majority might be spared to comfort and sustain the people of God, who were experiencing some very rough trials.

It is well known that Jeremiah's prediction came true all too soon. By 587 B.C. the unspeakable had become reality. Jerusalem was devastated. The temple was a huge pile of rubble. The Davidic king was stripped of his throne. The theology of Israel entered into a crisis stage. Its two major pillars had come crashing down. Jerusalem was no more. The Davidic dynasty was defeated. Everything popularly believed to be necessary for belief in God was gone.

The prophet Ezekiel inherited the task of interpreting this crisis. Why, it must often have been asked, should we serve a god who has just lost the last war? Why should we not run after Marduk, the god of Babylonia? After all, has he not conquered Yahweh, even as Yahweh himself earlier defeated the gods of Egypt and of Canaan? And since there is no holy city, no anointed king, no impressive temple, what is there to worship anyway? The answer of Ezekiel was clear. Yahweh himself caused the Exile. Marduk was merely a pawn in the hands of Yahweh to teach His people a lesson. Jeremiah was correct. Sin does lead to destruction. But wicked people who are being disciplined by God because of their wickedness may repent (Ezek. 33:19). And when they do, they will learn that the God who started the punishment can end it. In the famous metaphor of Ezekiel dry and lifeless bones *can* be resurrected (Ezek. 37:5–6). God can, and will, breathe divine Spirit into dry bones; He can and will call the four winds so to breathe into those bones that they come to life, stand erect, and form a vast army (v. 10).

The theological argument of Ezekiel must not be overlooked. God, he was arguing is not bound to a single place, even to Jerusalem. The Spirit of God is like the wind, which is capable of blowing wherever it pleases (John 3:8). And God can reach people whether they live in Jerusalem or in Babylon or anywhere else. No doubt this preaching from Ezekiel was largely responsible for the survival of faith among the Jews exiled from what they believed to be the country and the city of God, the place where He "lived."

But time was to bring another crisis. Even the preaching of Ezekiel pointed forward to the day when God would demonstrate His sovereignty once again by restoring dry bones, not only to life but also to the Promised Land (Ezek. 37:14, 24–28). Such a tenet would give rise to the question of chronology. *When* would the restoration occur? *How long* would the people of God have to languish in exile? Another prophet provided the answer:

> Comfort, comfort my people,
>   says your God.
> Speak tenderly to Jerusalem,
>   and proclaim to her
> that her hard service has been completed,
>   that her sin has been paid for,
> that she has received from the Lord's hand
>   double for all her sins.
>
>   (Isa. 40:1–2)

Here was a doctrine to meet the crisis of the moment. And what a doctrine it was! The second period of slavery, Isaiah preached, would end by means of a second exodus! "Forget the former things; do not dwell on the past. See, I [Yahweh] am doing a new thing!" (Isa. 43:18–19). Yet this *new thing* would be patterned after the *old thing* done in Egypt. Professor B. W. Anderson (see bibliography) has sketched ten motifs in the preaching of Isaiah concerning the release of the Jewish captives from Babylon that correspond to the major motifs of the Exodus from Egypt. These are as follows:

1. 40:3–5 — The highway in the wilderness.
2. 41:17–20 — The transformation of the wilderness.
3. 42:14–16 — Yahweh leads his people in a way they do not know.
4. 43:1–3 — Passing through the waters and the fire.
5. 43:14–21 — A way in the wilderness.
6. 48:20–21 — The exodus from Babylon.
7. 49:8–12 — The new entry into the Promised Land.
8. 51:9–10 — The new victory at the sea.
9. 52:11–12 — The new exodus.
10. 55:12–13 — Israel shall go out in joy and peace.

This relationship between the two exoduses was not altogether similar, however. In the case of their going out from Babylonian slavery, Yahweh did not encounter such stiff opposition from the ruler of that country as He had from the pharaoh of Egypt earlier. Rather, Cyrus, a Persian monarch, not only conquered the Babylonians but also cooperated with Yahweh in allowing Jews to return to their homeland. Although Cyrus did not acknowledge Yahweh (Isa. 45:4), he was performing the will of Israel's God throughout his career! In fact, he and Yahweh worked hand in hand (Isa. 45:1). Here once again is powerful testimony to the faith of the prophetic mind. Yahweh was not defeated. His people did not need to turn elsewhere for worship and sustenance. They needed only to realize the ways of their own Deity, Who was working to secure their release at a time when outward circumstances seemed to point in another direction.

The message in the Book of Isaiah proved correct. Cyrus did allow Jews (and other groups) to return to the lands from which they had been uprooted by the Babylonians. But this historical event was to precipitate yet another theological crisis for the Jews. Four factors lessened the impact of the decree of Cyrus on the minds and hearts of the Jews.

First, not everyone in Babylon wanted to return to Jerusalem. Life in Babylon had not been physically difficult. Freedom, within certain limits, had been permitted. And many Jews apparently had experienced material success in Babylon, and this made it difficult for them to agree to leave what they had worked for. Many of them had never seen Jerusalem. Many others had left it as small children. Virtually their entire way of life was Babylonian. Their language was not Hebrew but Aramaic, the language used in the Babylonian Empire for commercial communication. Their families and properties, no less than their memories and ways of life were bound up (or tied down!) in Babylon.

Second, those who did return found a less-than-perfect situation. The temple was still in ruins, the walls of the city were still down, and the former glory of Jerusalem was gone. In fact, even when the temple was being rebuilt, older people who remembered the splendor of Solomon's monument wept because of the inferiority of the second building (see Ezra 3:12). Later, efforts to repair the walls of the city also met mixed reaction. Rubble was so thick that work was thought to be impossible by some (Neh. 4:10). Opposition to the work was open and flagrant (vv. 1–3, 7–8). Many were forced to mortgage their possessions to buy food during a time of famine (Neh. 5:3). Others had to borrow money just to pay taxes (v. 4). It was necessary to work in shifts, half of the men standing guard while the other half worked (Neh. 4:16–18). Idealism was severely tested in the fires of reality. Only those with the clearest vision and the purest of motives persisted.

Third, the agricultural situation was difficult. The land of Palestine is rocky and sandy, yielding to the farmer even in good times only with a struggle. It is necessary to terrace the hills of the terrain carefully so as to preserve both soil and moisture. And during the period of the Exile no one had been on hand to nurse the soil through windstorms and heavy rains. No one had cared for the land, and the results were disastrous. Undoubtedly, growing decent crops was more difficult than anyone could have imagined before leaving Babylon. Additionally, the shortage of the number of people and the large size of the city to be repopulated (see Neh. 7:4) necessitated the loss of potential farmers and workers for the important enterprise of rebuilding the city and temple.

Fourth, there was internal dissension among those who had returned. Evidently, wealthier citizens had seized opportunities to lend money to poorer, or impoverished, persons. And these wealthy people had exacted usurious interest from the loans (Neh. 5:4–8). Even though they were all engaged in a common task, were all related by blood, and all had reason to fear enemies from outside their group, this did not prevent some from exploiting others whenever they could.

Now it is important to keep straight the sequence of the events discussed above with respect to the preaching of Malachi. If Malachi closely preceded Ezra and Nehemiah (as we assume that he did), all of the problems identified above from the book of Nehemiah were already flaring at their worst when Malachi addressed his audiences in Jerusalem. And it also means that Malachi's preaching did not succeed in converting Jerusalemites from their improper ways.

This situation also explains some other things related to the Book of Malachi. Under the conditions described above, is it any wonder that Malachi's audience thought it a shocking statement for a prophet to tell them of God's love (Mal. 1:2)? If indeed God loved them, why was it so terribly hard to wrestle a living from the rugged soil? Why were so many problems always looming ahead? Why? Why? Why?

Understanding the background of Malachi's audience also gives insight into the necessity for his sermons on the justice of God (see chapters 6 and 8). If God is fair, why do the evil prosper? Why does He allow cheating and gouging and usury? "Where is the God of justice?" (Mal. 2:17). Who would not be asking such questions!

In summary, then, the task of Malachi was to make sense—theological sense, but practical sense too—out of a crisis unprecedented in Israel's history. Unfortunately, Malachi has been relegated to the role of a "minor" prophet (because his book is so short). But in a way his task was comparable to that facing Jeremiah or Ezekiel or Isaiah of Babylon. How does one read the past with its record of God's faithfulness in redemption? How does one interpret the present with its problems and its questions? And how does one synthesize the past and the present in a creative and yet theologically responsible fashion? Malachi must be given high marks indeed for his answers to these important questions.

G. The Formation of a Book of Prophecy

Over the years scholars from various theological persuasions have debated about the books of prophecy that now appear in the Christian Bible. One of the basic issues in these debates has been centered around the way our biblical books of prophecy actually came into their present shape. That is, what steps were involved in the development of prophetic messages from the original, oral form in which they were preached by an individual prophet to the written books now contained in the Bible?

To begin our discussion of this process, two extreme positions may be overruled. On the one hand, there have been scholars who have argued that every word now found in a book bearing the name of a particular prophet must be attributed in mechanical fashion to that prophet and to no other person. In other words, every single word in the Book of Isaiah must have been spoken by Isaiah. Otherwise, the argument runs, the entire Bible is laid open to question, and it may perhaps not be trusted in other matters. On the other hand, scholars operating with different sets of presuppositions have argued for the opposite extreme and have systematically denied virtually the whole of the present books of prophecy to those persons whose names they now bear. It must be repeated that neither of these extreme positions has borne the weight of scrutiny.

With respect to the latter opinion, it is fair to say that no competent scholar today is as negative regarding the participation of prophets such as Isaiah and Ezekiel in the books bearing their names as was almost commonly the case a few decades ago. No one is attempting to deny the existence of the great prophets or their contributions to the books with which they are identified by tradition. With respect to the former position, it is accurate to note that exponents of this extremely hard line, or literalistic view, have seldom been lacking. In this regard there is a very basic misconception that needs to be corrected. One need not be willing to attribute uncritically every word in the Isaiah *book* to Isaiah of Jerusalem or every word in the Malachi *book* to a prophet now known as Malachi in order to qualify for the kingdom of heaven. The excessive claims of overly zealous exponents of this kind of fundamentalism notwithstanding, many devout and sincere Christians have chosen another alternative.

Perhaps the issue may be brought more sharply into focus by asking a simple question. What is involved in believing that someone other than the master prophet named by a particular book was connected with the composition of the final, biblical form of that book? The position taken in this commentary is that the biblical evidence itself supports the idea that persons other than Isaiah, Jeremiah, Ezekiel, and Malachi, etc., were indeed instrumental in bringing the various prophetic books to their final, canonical form. At least three points deserve consideration in support of this position.

Attention should be given first of all to the opening verses of the "named" books of prophecy. Typically, certain kinds of information are included in these introductory verses: the date of the prophet's ministry calculated in relation to a king's reign or other significant event; the names of the kings under whose reign the prophet preached; a brief genealogical identification of the prophet; the location of the prophet's sphere of activity. In plain terms this is information given from someone other than the prophet about the person whose name is to be attached to the book. It is information written *about* the prophet whose messages follow, but not necessarily written *by* that prophet, and it is certainly not presented to the public as if it were part of the prophet's actual messages. As a matter of fact, these opening verses (and many others) appear almost certainly to have been written by people who lived sometime after the career of the prophet himself. More than anything else, these "superscriptions" are attempts to evaluate and accredit the work of the earlier prophet for a community of the faithful who lived after his actual lifetime (see further on Malachi 1:1 in chapter 2).

Second, we know that at least some of the outstanding prophets gathered disciples around themselves. These "sons of the prophets" studied under the great master and attempted to emulate and preserve his work after he had died. Sometimes a single successor would be chosen from among the larger group; he might even become famous in his own right, as did Elisha in the wake of the powerful Elijah (see 1 Kings 19:19–21; 2 Kings 2:1–15). More often, the actual successor to the master remained anonymous. But in either case the role of the disciples was understood to be primarily that of continuing the work begun by the great leader. Whatever issues the master prophet had debated during his lifetime, whatever social stands he may have taken, whatever ethical positions he may have enunciated—all were to be preserved and transmitted to subsequent generations of disciples. In attempting to keep alive the purposes of the master, no doubt these later disciples involved themselves in commenting on his original words for the purpose of updating them and of maintaining their relevancy in each succeeding era. Sometimes the prophet's words about a given issue were to be recorded and preserved in secret among his followers until an appropriate time for their publication (see Isa. 8:16). Sometimes the messages of a prophet were revised and expanded within his own lifetime (see Jer. 36:32).

The point is that the master prophets, whom we have come to know so well from the records of Scripture, did not minister and study alone, isolated from the rest of society. They made disciples, taught younger persons their views, even headed academies or seminarylike organizations (as 2 Kings 6:1–7 indicates). And the devoted students and co-workers with the prophet participated in his ministry in substantive ways. We should not, therefore, be surprised to discover that a brilliant pupil might add to the original message of the great master a few words of explanation that would commend the truth previously taught by his mentor to a current generation. Indeed, this act of updating, of making relevant, and of relating biblical truth to current problems is really the goal of biblical preaching in every generation down to the present.

There is a third issue that must be considered here too. It should not be supposed that every word ever spoken by any single prophet has been preserved in the Bible. The Gospel of John specifically testifies that not all the words and deeds of Jesus were recorded (see John 21:25). And if a three-year ministry could not be recorded in full, how much more difficult would such a recording task be for the longer careers of most of the prophets of Israel! Isaiah, for example, probably enjoyed a career of more than forty years' duration. And even Malachi, whose book is far smaller than the Isaiah book, doubtless preached more than the six sermons that have been preserved in the biblical record. It becomes obvious, therefore that someone must have been involved in the process of sorting through the materials left by a given prophet for the purpose of determining which messages should be published in written form, which should be used in oral form in the seminary classroom, and which probably did not need to be repeated. Furthermore, recent studies are showing ever more clearly that the books of prophecy are arranged in detailed and quite intricate structural patterns that simply could not have happened by chance. Someone arranged the prophet's various messages that had been chosen for inclusion in book form. And this arrangement was sometimes topical, sometimes chronological, and sometimes related to the literary genres that had been used for different messages.

In the course of a lifetime of ministry each prophet might preach about a variety of subjects. Social problems, political events, and many other things would demand his attention at one time or another. To take only one of many possible examples, no one should suppose that Jeremiah preached all of his sermons against foreign nations at the same time or in the sequence in which they now appear in the Jeremiah book. When six consecutive chapters of the Jeremiah book (46–51) are devoted to this one issue of foreign nations, the most obvious conclusion appears to be that someone carefully selected representative works from the available sermons and speeches of Jeremiah and placed them together in one section of the book. These sermons are certainly those that the editor believed to be most representative of Jeremiah's position on foreign nations. But as we have seen, Jeremiah probably gave other similar speeches that were excluded from the biblical work in its present form. As a matter of fact, these chapters are arranged differently in the Septuagint version of Jeremiah in clear testimony to the fact that there were at least two editorial views concerning them.

Perhaps a better way to say what has been argued above is as follows. Someone had to copy down the words of a sermon that had been preached. Someone had to preserve these and similar words. Someone had to select from the larger corpus of a prophet's works those pieces that were suited for transmission to subsequent groups of students and disciples. Someone had to arrange and edit the final shape of these materials to make them readable and meaningful for later generations. And at least at some point, early or late after the death of the master prophet, the process had to end with a favorable consensus from the disciples and their intended audience. Perhaps it is conceivable that for each book a single person was responsible for all of the steps outlined above. But it is more likely that a long period of time was needed and that many different generations of disciples were involved in the total process from oral sermon to written biblical book.

We are left with few real clues about this process.

That almost all of these copiers and preservers and selectors and arrangers and editors have remained anonymous is an additional problem for our culture because we long to know exactly who is responsible for every bit of writing, acting, directing, producing, etc., in a modern drama. But such anonymity was not a problem for the ancient disciples. In their minds everything they were doing was secondary in importance to the task of allowing generation after generation to hear and respond to the inspired messages of the master. As long as his name was remembered, they believed that they were doing their job well.

It is proper to address a final question at this point. What does such a view do to one's doctrine of the inspiration and the authority of the Bible? Often it has been claimed that to believe in an inspired Bible is to believe that a single inspired individual spoke and wrote everything that current and later generations associated with his name. But this argument misses the point. Of course, Isaiah was inspired. So were Jeremiah, Ezekiel, and all the other prophets. But the Spirit of God was not absent from the hearts and minds of those who carefully considered the question of what to preserve and what to leave aside. These people, too, must have been guided divinely unless the growth of the biblical canon be attributed to merely human causes. What is needed is a doctrine of inspiration that is broad enough to include *all* of the people who were involved in the making of the biblical books at every point along the line. An inspired speaker is the proper beginning point, to be sure. But also necessary are an inspired community to receive the messages as Scripture. And in between the beginning and the end we must also affirm that divine guidance and wisdom were given to the disciples who copied, preserved, arranged, selected, and edited in final form what became the Bible.

If this broader view is adopted, it is not nearly so crucial to our faith if it is decided that a particular verse in a prophetic book was not actually part of the messages of the original master prophet but rather an explanatory or editorial comment *about* the original message. And it will no longer be necessary to denounce persons whose views about these kinds of verses are different from our own, for it was the form of the books as we now have them—including original messages, editorial framework, explanatory comments, and everything else—that both Judaism and Christianity declared to be Scripture (the Canon). We should, rather, thank God for each piece of information that has been included in the Scriptures. Perhaps the comments of a faithful disciple living later than the master prophet may point us in the correct direction for attempting to make those same messages relevant for our own times. But it must be emphasized that it is the prophetic books in their entirety that are canonical. And it is as whole books that they point the way to an understanding of God, of ourselves, and of all things necessary for salvation.

As we begin to study Malachi, these points must be remembered. Not all of Malachi's sermons have been preserved. Perhaps the sequence in which the six that remain were originally preached has been altered in the published form that we now study. Nevertheless, we are given to understand that the six sermons now contained in the Malachi book were believed to represent fairly the total ministry of the prophet. To study these sermons is, according to the community that recognized and received them as Scripture, to know the spirit and the essence of Malachi. Even as the *Standard Sermons* of John Wesley must be the starting point in the attempt to understand the man and his message, these six sermons are Malachi's *Standard Sermons*. And what they have to say has stood the test of time. That is, we must no longer say simply that these messages (and all other parts of the Bible too) were *inspired* and that therefore they are authoritative. We must realize that the process worked the other way historically. Because these words were observed by the people of God to function authoritatively and changingly in people's lives, they recognized them as having been inspired.

For Further Study

1. What is the significance of the Book of Malachi for you? What difference has it ever made in your life?

2. What is the most significant theological problem facing the people of God today? Do you think there are any prophets around who might create fresh approaches from Scripture to help deal with this problem?

3. How do you feel about the theory of the composition of a biblical book presented here? Does it bother you to think that several people need to have been inspired rather than one individual alone?

4. Do you agree that the Bible is a book that belongs to the community of faith? How does this affect your own personal interpretations of it?

Chapter 2

The Superscription
(Malachi 1:1)

The first verse of the Book of Malachi, called a superscription, is similar in many ways to the first verse of many other prophetic books in the Bible. However, this verse in Malachi also contains significant differences from other superscriptions, and these differences are important enough to demand some attention in interpretation before studying the bulk of the book that follows.

The New International Version translates Malachi 1:1 as follows: "An oracle: The word of the LORD to Israel through Malachi." This is merely a standard way to render the verse, but as I will show, it does not do full justice to the thought that lies behind the addition of the verse to the messages of Malachi.

In order to understand the Malachian superscription, a quick look at the superscriptions of several other prophetic books is quite instructive. After examining several of these other superscriptions, it will be readily apparent that there are two very important words that occur together in Malachi 1:1. Usually one *or* the other is used in a superscription; it is quite rare in books of prophecy for both words to be used together in the same verse (but see Zech. 9:1 and 12:1). These two words are *Massa'* and *davar*.

The Hebrew word *massa'*, translated by NIV as "oracle," has a very definite function in prophetic language. The root of the noun *massa'* is the verb *nasa'*, which means "to pick up" or "to carry." A *massa'* is, accordingly, something picked up or carried, and this explains its translation in several English versions of the Bible as being "burden" or "load." Now the noun *massa'* itself is used frequently within the prophetic books to refer to the burden that the prophet believed he was called on by God to carry on behalf of the people, and to deliver from God to those people. Hence, the translation of the word as "oracle" by NIV places the emphasis on the proclamation aspect of the prophet's assignment rather than on other aspects such as the role of intercessor. However, it should not be forgotten that the Hebrew word *massa'* carries *both* ideas, "burden" and "oracle," rather than one to the exclusion of the other.

Clearly, we need not conclude that the editor considered a divine assignment to have been a burden for the prophet in the totally negative sense of the term (though for Jeremiah it seemed to be!). Rather, we should understand the description of a prophet's work to mean an acknowledgment of the responsibility that was his in *carrying* a message from God to His people. Certainly in Malachi 1:1 *massa'* is so employed.

Still, we have not begun to plumb the depths of the meaning of *massa'* merely by translating it even in such a broad and inclusive fashion as described above. We must notice for the purpose of comparison the superscription of Habakkuk, in which *massa'* is used in a very instructive way. That is, if we examine the way in which *massa'* is used in the opening verse of Habakkuk, we will get a better idea about the way it functions in Malachi 1:1. We may translate the opening words of Habakkuk as "the *massa'* that the prophet Habakkuk saw." That is, Habakkuk's *massa'* was received by means of a special vision. Because this verse is placed at the very beginning of the entire collection of the messages of Habakkuk, we are given to understand that what follows in the book is a description of what a certified prophet had received by vision from God for the people Israel. In other words, the term *massa'* in Habakkuk 1:1 means almost precisely what the English word *revelation* has come to mean in twentieth-century speech. Surely the use of *massa'* in Malachi 1:1 must be understood in the same vein, even though no information has been given in this case about the methods by which the prophet obtained these insights from God. Still, in practical terms we should observe that in place of NIV's opening translation ("An oracle:"), we may understand the following: "What you are about to read [in this book known as Malachi] is divine revelation [*massa'*]!"

With this understanding of the Hebrew word *massa'*, we may turn to an examination of the second significant word, the Hebrew word *davar*. Here, as very often elsewhere in the prophets, *davar* occurs in conjunction with another word, *Yahweh*, to form a standard idea: *Yahweh-davar* (NIV: "The word of the LORD").

In the Hebrew Scriptures there are four standard formulas, all of which use *davar* either in a superscription or to introduce individual prophetic sayings within the body of a prophetic book. These four formulas are as follows:

1. "Now a *davar* from Yahweh came to [a personal name]." This formula is used in Jonah 1:1; 2 Samuel 7:4; 1 Kings 6:11; 12:22; 13:20; 16:1; 21:17; 21:28; Zechariah 7:8; Haggai 1:3; and numerous times throughout the lengthy Book of Jeremiah.

2. "*Davar* from Yahweh came to [a personal name]." Examples of this formula may be seen in Zechariah 1:1; Ezekiel 1:3; and Haggai 1:1.

3. "Came a *davar* from Yahweh to [a personal name]." This formula merely reverses the order of the verb and subject from that found in the second formula and is illustrated in 2 Samuel 24:11 and 1 Kings 18:1.

4. "A *davar* came from Yahweh that came to [a personal name]." Examples of this formula are found in the superscriptions of Hosea, Joel, Micah, and Zephaniah.

Why? Why this frequent employment of *davar* to describe the prophetic ministry in ancient Israel? And why is the formula in each case limited to the expression "a *davar* from Yahweh"? It has often been noted by biblical scholars that the Hebrew word *davar* means either a "word" or a "thing," either something that is spoken or something that is done. Highlighted here is the common connection in Hebrew thought between what someone *says* and what that person *does*. To speak a word was to give life to an idea, virtually to create something by saying it. That is why, for example, it was crucial that the professional Balaam be prevented from uttering (saying) a curse against Israel (see Num. 22–24). Even to utter the curse that he had been hired to pronounce against Israel would give existence to the idea that Israel could be defeated. So he must not be allowed to speak such an idea for fear that he might thus actually create it, give it life, which would grant it validity. In short, for Balaam to *speak* of defeat for Israel might *cause* that defeat. Thus, the interpreters of this intriguing event carefully state that Balaam was not allowed to utter his curse because the God of Israel forbade him to do so (see Num. 22:38)!

Even a cursory survey of the ways in which *davar* is used in the

Hebrew Scriptures illustrates this duality between saying and doing. For example, in Genesis 24 the aged Abraham sent forth his trusty servant to obtain a proper wife for the beloved son Isaac. For sixty-five verses the narrator skillfully describes the adventures of the servant: his journey, his silent prayers of meditation, his meeting with the woman of destiny, his conversation with her family, etc. Finally, in verse 66 of the chapter, the servant's mission was accomplished. The heroine had been brought back safely, and a joyous wedding was soon to be celebrated.

Naturally, the servant was anxious to report exactly all of his experiences. Genesis 24:66 describes his report in the following way: "Then the servant reported to Isaac all the *devarim* (plural of *davar*) that he had accomplished" (CDI). There it is! The servant had spoken many *words* in lengthy negotiations with the family of the bride. But he also had done many *things* in the carrying out of his mission. *Davar* is used to describe both. That is what is meant by the duality of meaning carried by *davar*.

There is, however, a much more specific function that *davar* performs in biblical literature. This more technical role may be illustrated by reference to its use in 1 Samuel 3:1 and 3:21. In 3:1 we are told that during the early life of Samuel the *davar* of the Lord was rarely given. From the context it is clear that this expression refers to a period of spiritual famine in the land of ancient Israel, a time during which truth from God or instructions from God for living were absent from the people. The gist of the ensuing story is that the period of scarcity of prophetic revelation was ended by the gracious decision of Yahweh to appear (reveal himself) in Shiloh to the obedient and faithful lad Samuel. In fact, the precise expression that is employed in 3:21 indicates plainly that the spiritual famine had ended "because Yahweh was revealed to Samuel in Shiloh, by means of the *davar* of Yahweh" (CDI).

The *davar* of Yahweh, then, referred to the entire scope of the revelatory process in which Yahweh became involved for the purpose of giving his truth to Israel through Samuel (who in 3:20 is identified as a prophet). Or to say it another way, the *davar* of Yahweh was the *medium* of revelation from Yahweh through Samuel to Israel. Yahweh was known through His *davar*, both in word and in deed!

It is this specialized meaning of the word *davar* that must be kept in mind in interpreting passages such as the apparently simple first verse of Malachi. In reality, whenever the biblical editors spoke of the *davar* of Yahweh, they implied their belief that divine truth was involved. As seen earlier, this is basically the impact of the word *massa'* as well.

As noted in the Introduction, it is commonly agreed among biblical scholars that the superscriptions of the prophetic books are not part of the actual messages of the prophets. They represent, rather, the editorial judgment of persons living at a later time, whose responsibility it was to compile and transmit the prophetic materials that were available to them. Probably the editors responsible for adding the superscriptions to the prophetic books reflected the view held commonly by people in their own era, whenever that may have been. But, to say the least, the *official* view of the prophetic books that is presented by the(se) editor(s) is that the messages that have been preserved from older prophets were more than mere sermons from an ordinary person. They were, in point of fact, nothing less than divine truth from Yahweh. They were revelation. Only such an understanding explains fully the significance of the use of words like *massa'* and *davar* in books like Malachi.

Therefore, we must think in the following terms. While it is true that each of the messages contained in the Book of Malachi has a specific historical situation out of which it originated and to which it was addressed, it is also true that subsequent generations of Israelites believed those same messages were applicable and appropriate to their own day. These later generations are witnesses of the ability of the truths of Malachi to function in redeeming, revealing, saving ways for the community of faith over extended periods of time. This criterion of functionality is a large part of what is meant by saying that Malachi belongs in the canon of sacred Scripture, not only for Jews in and subsequent to the era of Malachi but also for Christians even down to the present day. In every case it was and is as special revelation from Yahweh that Malachi continued to be studied and preached in synagogue and church alike.

In addition to *massa'* and *davar*, there is a third very special word that appears in the superscription to the Book of Malachi. It is the Hebrew word YHWH, pronounced Yahweh. Unfortunately, this word has been badly misunderstood or improperly rendered in various translations of the Bible from early times. It should be remembered above all that the word YHWH is in Hebrew a *proper name*, the specific name of the particular and unique Deity who was the God of

Israel. But in English YHWH is most often translated as "LORD" (e.g., RSV, NIV), and this makes it difficult for English readers to understand that what appears in their language to be a title or even a common noun (a lord) is, in fact, a Hebrew proper name, Yahweh. Along with this we may note that a related word that functions as a *proper* noun in English is really a *common* noun or an adjective in the Hebrew language. This is the Hebrew word *'elohim,* which comes into English as "God."

The Hebrew word *'elohim* is used to refer not only to the God of Israel but also to the gods of Egypt, Canaan, Babylonia, Assyria, and so forth. What this means is that in English we reverse the mode of thought implied by the Hebrew usage. YHWH becomes a common noun rather than a proper noun and a specific name, while *'elohim* is viewed as a definite proper noun translated "God."

The confusion that results from this English turnaround may be illustrated by reference to a familiar verse in Psalm 33:12, which contains the following statement: "Blessed is the nation whose *'elohim* is Yahweh." Most English versions (including NIV) translate this sentence into something like this: "Blessed is the nation whose God [capital "G"!] is the Lord" (NIV). But no nation except Israel had only one deity; implying that to say that *'elohim* means the one and only God is wide of the mark. What the psalmist was trying to affirm was somewhat different. His idea was plain enough. Any nation that desires to be blessed must realize that it can achieve this end only by means of choosing Yahweh as its deity. This could easily be indicated in English by saying, "Blessed is the nation whose *deity* is Yahweh." It was the presence of Yahweh among the people of Israel that afforded them the blessings of life. Any group of people desiring similar blessings should expect it from no deity other than this same Yahweh, who is the special Divinity of Israel.

We must keep all of this "God talk" in mind as we return to Malachi 1:1 to notice that everything learned about the unique meaning of *massa'* and *davar* as "revelation" makes sense only when it is coupled with Israel's belief that the revelation came from Yahweh. His *davar* alone is true. Revelation, as ancient Israel understood it, came not through gods but through Yahweh alone. Therefore, to say that what we are about to read in Malachi is special revelation from Yahweh was the editor's way of asserting the highest possible authority for the book.

But we are informed in the superscription of something more. Hand in hand with this triple emphasis on the character of prophetic truth as being divine revelation, we are told also that this revelation from the unique Deity of Israel was mediated "by the hand of," or "through," (NIV) Malachi. This phrase, too, is significant. We have noted the view of the editor that the Book of Malachi is divine revelation from Yahweh. But to say that such revelation comes through human beings is equally important. Revelation did not occur in a mysterious, or an extraearthly, fashion. It came through a person. Audiences saw and heard a normal man speaking an understandable and common language. The personality of the prophet was not squelched, nor was his uniqueness as an individual vetoed. He was allowed to express things his own way (compare, for example, the differences in style between Amos and Hosea, or between Paul and Peter in New Testament times).

While we must never forget that the burden of Malachi was viewed as divine truth-revelation, neither should we forget that God used an ordinary human being as the medium through which that very *un*ordinary revelation was given.

A Final Note

Already in the comments on the superscription, reference has been made to "Malachi" as if an actual person were intended. This is the simplest way to handle references to the book. Though it is to be understood, as noted above, that the Hebrew word *mal'akhi* is a title rather than the name of a specific person who wrote a book that now bears his name, it is still convenient to follow tradition and use "Malachi" as a personal name.

For Further Study

1. What is your view of the messages of Malachi? Are they still divine revelation for you even though they are found in the Old Testament?

2. Does it bother you to think that God has chosen someone who was apparently quite ordinary to deliver the messages we now know as Malachi?

3. Are you bothered to learn that we really do not know who "Malachi" was or anything else about his life and work?

4. How would you translate Malachi 1:1?

Chapter 3

The Love of God and the Hatred of God
(Malachi 1:2–5)

Strong Statement: "'I have loved you,' says the Lord" (v. 2a).

Anticipated Question: "How?" (v. 2b).

Elaboration: The Example of Jacob and Esau (vv. 2c–5).

A. The Problem

In this paragraph Malachi addresses the problem of the love and the hatred (or the favor and the disfavor) of God that may be deduced from history. Two statements made by Yahweh appear to be quite contradictory in logical terms. How could the same Deity declare, "I have loved Jacob" and "I have hated Esau"? The answer must be sought by means of careful interpretation of this paragraph in context, with respect to the original setting and force of the utterance, and in light of Scripture as a whole.

1. *Extreme statements a literary device*

In Hebrew thought, statements that appear extreme to the modern Western mind are often made. They serve a definite literary purpose that is not intended to be taken in a literal fashion. Even in the New Testament these kinds of extreme statements are found. For example, Jesus said to a large crowd of people, "If anyone comes to me and does not hate his father and mother, his wife and children, his brothers and sisters—yes, even his own life—he cannot be my disciple" (Luke 14:26). But no one should suppose for a moment that Jesus expected people to hate their parents and family in the literal sense of the word *hate* as it functions in modern English. What He was calling for was complete obedience to the kingdom of God.

A similar understanding of the context must be used in reading the statements attributed to Yahweh in Malachi 1:2–3. Yahweh's "hatred" for the Edomites was not a childish or a vindictive human emotion. The point is rather that the love that God had exhibited toward Israel (Jacob) becomes indisputable when one begins to compare even the unhappy fortunes of Jews with the far worse fate of the Edomites. It is in comparison with his relationship to Israel that God's relationship with Esau seems stern indeed.

2. Covenantal relationships

Another consideration is necessary for a proper understanding of these divine statements. The words *love* and *hate* are used throughout the Old Testament to describe covenantal relationships. An excellent illustration of this fact is provided by Genesis 26. Early in the chapter Isaac began to have trouble with Abimelech and his Philistine compatriots (vv. 14–15). This led Abimelech to order Isaac to move away from the area (v. 16). After experiencing similar troubles with the local populace in Gerar (vv. 17–22), Isaac moved at last to Beersheba (v. 23). At some point after this move Abimelech paid a visit to Isaac, seeking a way to make peace with him (v. 26). Naturally, Isaac wondered about Abimelech's reasons or motives for coming. "'Why,'" he asked, 'have you come to me, since you were [earlier] hostile to me and sent me away?'" (v. 27). Now the clause that the NIV has translated, "You were hostile to me" employs exactly the same word that is translated "hate" in Malachi 1:3. What Isaac said literally was the statement "You hated me!"

The development of the story from this point on illustrates the real function of the word *hate* in the Old Testament. In response to the question of Isaac, Abimelech admitted that because of the clear evidence that Isaac was blessed by God he (Abimelech) and his Philistine fellow citizens saw the need to enter into a *covenant* relationship with him (Isaac). That is, the people who had earlier "hated" Isaac, who had had no legal or nonaggression pact with him, now desired to be at peace with him because of his evident prosperity. Nor should their "hatred" of Isaac at the first be taken to imply petulance and childish emotion. He was an outsider who lacked a legal agreement covering land and resource utilization with the natives. But once a covenant was obtained, they were able to live with him in peace and had no further reason to "hate" him.

In addition to the range of ideas normally associated with love, the Hebrew word for "love" functions in much the same way in the rest of Old Testament literature as in the story of Isaac. To love someone was to be involved with him or her in a mutually binding, legal agreement (covenant).

This knowledge of the range of meaning both for love and for hate in the Old Testament can help us to understand the paragraph at hand from Malachi. The love of God for Jacob, as well as the hatred of God for Esau, may be demonstrated to rest on historical reality. Yahweh and Israel had long understood their relationship together as covenantal in nature. But the Edomites had never consented to enter into covenant with Yahweh. Rather, according to prophetic accusations Esau had had an outrageous, totally unacceptable life style by any standard (see for example Amos 1:11). Acts of crime flew in the face of normal and widely accepted ideas of social and political performance. Their life style meant that they could not possibly be in league with the God Who desired to be known as the champion of justice and of fair play for all persons. In short, Yahweh did "hate" Esau, even as it could be said that Esau "hated" Yahweh. Nothing bound the two parties together.

3. *To make a point*

Yet another point needs to be made here in evaluating these statements about God's love and the hatred of God. Malachi was speaking to an audience that was decidedly hostile to him and apparently in no mood at all to be told that God cared for (loved) them. Their rebuilt temple was but a shadow of their "real," or first one. Their political independence was gone. Their future was cloudy in many areas (see the Introduction). Into this mind-set, therefore, the stark reality of the horrible fate of Edom was used by the prophet to hammer home to his audience the point that Yahweh's dealings with them had been demonstrably more favorable than with some of their closest neighbors.

B. The Contrast in Pronouns

The antithesis between the words *love* and *hate* is not the only point of contrast in the paragraph. In terms of literary structure, one other contrasting idea is readily apparent. It is the contrast that is signaled by the positioning and the functioning of three different pronouns throughout the paragraph: I (referring to Yahweh), you (referring to the

Israelites), and they (referring to the Edomites). Notice the following:

Yahweh	*Israel*	*Edom*
I have loved	*you* ask	
I have hated		
I have wasted		*they* may say
		they may rebuild
I will demolish		
	you will see	
	you will say	

These pronouns and the verbs they are used with serve to emphasize the sovereignty of Yahweh as set over against the limitations of both Israel and Edom. Over against the questioning "Why?" of the Israelites stands the authority of the God of Israel to declare in forthright terms His love for His people. Over against the resolution of the shattered Edomites to rebuild their country and their lives stands the sovereign Lord of Israel and of the world—the One Who is free to declare His intention to tear down everything Edom is capable of rebuilding.

We may paraphrase the ideas thus presented as follows: *You* (Israel) may question My love, but *I* declare it still. *They* (Edom) may doubt My ability to ruin them for their sins, but *I* will surely act in accordance with My original intention to destroy them utterly.

C. The Usage of the Verb "To Say"

The importance of the two major contrasts in the paragraph notwithstanding, there is another vocabulary word that is used throughout the verses to signal *the* primary idea of the prophet. It is the Hebrew word *'amar*, meaning "to say." Five times *'amar* is used in verses 2–5, and although it is an extremely common word in the Old Testament, in this particular paragraph it performs a rather *un*common task.

The opening statement, "I have loved you," (v. 2) is something that Yahweh *said ('amar)*. In quick response Israel threw down a challenge to His assertion. What the NIV translates (properly for stylistic reasons) as the clause "But you *ask*" is a second occurrence of the word *'amar;* it means literally, "But you *say!*" That is, what Yahweh had said was not accepted by Israel. Against His saying, a saying of the people was advanced. "I have loved you," *said* Yahweh. "Prove it," *said* the people. Again the idea of the sovereignty of God lies close at hand. Does He have the right to make such a bold statement to people who are suffering and depressed? Do they have the right to challenge His alleged love? That is the issue.

The next occurrences of '*amar* are in verse 4. Once again the saying of Yahweh is set over against what human beings may attempt to say on their own authority. "Edom may *say*, '. . . we will rebuild." But in sharpest contrast are the words "This is what the Lord [Yahweh] Almighty *says:* 'They may build, but I will demolish.'" Here it is the saying of the Edomites that is contrasted with the saying of Yahweh. How strange that the people of the covenant were doing essentially the same thing of which the Edomites were adjudged guilty: they were *saying* the opposite of what Yahweh had declared about Himself and about them. Their circumstances differed enormously from those of Israel, but in the matter of disagreeing with Yahweh, Edom and Israel were too much alike.

It is the final use of '*amar* that resolves the tension between people and Deity, between human *saying* and divine *saying*. The actions of the sovereign Lord (Yahweh) would come to be observed by the people of Israel in such plain terms that there could be no mistaking His majesty and power. Hence, verse 5 reads thus: "You [Israelites] will see it [My activity among the Edomites] with your own eyes and *say* [!], 'Great is the LORD [Yahweh]—even beyond the borders of Israel!'" The only proper resolution of the problem is for the people of God to begin to speak correctly about Him as evidence of the fact that they have perceived correctly the meaning of His working in the world. His greatness must be affirmed, and once that issue is settled, His authority to declare His love, hatred, or anything else will be assured.

It is necessary here to recall the earlier discussion about the relationship in Hebrew thought between *word* and *thing* or between *saying* and *doing*. In a very real sense, what the people were saying was symptomatic of what they really were and of the way they were living. And so it was with Yahweh, too. The One who *said*, "I have loved," could also be seen to *act* in love if anyone were bothering to look. Although those who hated Him would learn well of His wrath, to those who would love Him and keep His commandments, He would certainly show His own love in response (see Exod. 20:5–6!).

D. The Status of Israel

There is a final idea that must be noted in this opening paragraph of the Book of Malachi. The significance of affirming that the greatness of Yahweh would someday be recognized "even beyond the borders of Israel" (v. 5) contains a distinct note of hope and promise. One of the ways in which the relationship between Yahweh and Israel was expressed to the world was dependent on the status of Israel among the other nations in the international community. Israel was known as the people of Yahweh; so if Yahweh could not take care of (prosper) His own people, who could believe that all other nations should seek Him as their Deity too!

This idea may also be inverted, for if the greatness of Yahweh was being acknowledged abroad, it could only be because at home, *within* the borders of Israel, things were going well. This is the element of hope. However hard Edom might attempt to rebuild, for her there was no hope. Yahweh would simply tear down her feeble efforts. But it was to be different for Israel. Someday her God would be acknowledged as the true Ruler of the world. What Israel would rebuild (while returning His love for her), Yahweh would protect.

To people whose *present* is less than perfect, whether they be a fifth-century audience hearing Malachi or a twentieth-century congregation seeking the words of God for their day, the hope for a brighter future is an abiding and sustaining one indeed. In the thinking of Malachi, nothing could be more hopeful than the thought that the God whom he served would come in due time to be exalted throughout the world.

For Further Study

1. In a Bible dictionary or a Bible encyclopedia (listed in the bibliography), read the articles on Edom and Esau. Notice the places in the Old Testament where these two are discussed. Was there good reason for God to "hate" them?

2. Would it be correct in our culture to say that God hates people who are not "Israelites" or members of the church? If not, how should the attitude of God toward these "outsiders" or nonbelievers be described?

3. What is your view of the sovereignty of God? How does this view affect your day-to-day life?

Chapter 4

The Sins of the Priests
(Malachi 1:6–2:9)

There are several "Strong Statements" in this rather lengthy discourse about the priesthood in ancient Israel. Notice that several verses mention exceptionally unacceptable statements, attitudes, or actions implemented by the priests (vv. 6–7, 12–13; 2:8). This multiplicity of strong statements should mean, of course, that there are also several "Anticipated Questions." In fact, though, there are only two such questions placed on the lips of the priests: "How have we despised your [God's] name" (1:6) and "How have we defiled you?" (1:7). This indicates rather clearly that the issue the prophet wished to discuss was related to the concept of *ritual purity in the practice of correct worship of God.* His accusation of the priests may thus be boiled down to the single matter of defilement (of their service, their attitudes, and the utensils used in their worship). The "Elaboration" is far more extensive than that contained in the first paragraph, which spoke of God's love and His hatred. It was expected that the priests would take seriously the business of worshiping God. For them to take sacred matters lightly was the worst sin imaginable.

A. The Importance of Doing God's Business Correctly (1:6–14)

1. *A matter of honor (1:6)*

The word *honor* jumps immediately to the fore in the first statement concerning the problem of which the prophet wishes to accuse the priests. Fathers and masters received honor from their sons or their servants as a matter of course. It was just that way. Society demanded it. Custom prescribed it. The very orderliness of the community depended on it. Indeed, the official legislation of the ancient Israelites spoke unambiguously to these dual emphases. For example, Deuteronomy 21:18–21 stipulated that any son who continued to be disobedient to his parents, after all attempts to correct him had failed, had to be put to death. This prescription of capital punishment surely underscores the importance placed by the society of that day on sons granting respect and obedience to their fathers and mothers. This prescription provides the background against which this opening statement of Malachi must be understood. It was simply expected and assumed that a son would honor his father.

There is another piece of background information about ancient Israelite society that serves to clarify this particular method of reasoning. One of the happiest and favorite ways of describing Israel's relationship to God was the custom of calling Him Father. Thus Psalm 68:5 describes God as a Father to the fatherless. Deuteronomy 32:6 refers to God as the Father and the Creator of Israel. Hosea 11:1 views the beginning of God's dealings with Israel in Egypt as a Father-son relationship. The brilliant Jeremiah portrays God as One Who assumed that His people would call Him their Father (3:19), and he uses words that indicate God's feeling in the matter by quoting Him as saying how greatly He longed to restore His people to an abundant life "because I [God] am Israel's father" (31:9). Of course, the counterpart to this idea of God's being their Father is that the people of Israel often delighted in referring to themselves as God's sons.

Such information shows just how shattering the accusation of Malachi would be to the priests, who prided themselves on being the elite among the people (sons) of God. They were guilty of withholding from God the most basic right of any father—honor. Notice carefully the NIV rendering of the two questions that Malachi has God ask the priests: (1) "Where is the honor due me?" and (2) "Where is the respect due me?" (v. 6). Honor and respect were indeed the due, the legal right of a father or a master.

All of this would have been bad enough in and of itself. But Malachi does not say only that the priests were guilty of a sin of *omission* (failure to honor God properly); he continues his indictment by asserting that they were also guilty of a terrible sin of *comission*. "It is you, O priests, who despise my name" (v. 6). Now *honor* and *despise* function in this verse as polar opposites. As we will see, *despise* is a word to which Malachi returns in subsequent verses. In his first use of it he clearly intends to say that the priests had not simply grown lax in a harmless way, no longer honoring God in external ways that could be observed. No, what they were doing to God was deliberately done. Theoretically, one could fail to honor a country or a custom in a specific way simply as an oversight. One might forget, for example, to salute the flag or to stand when the national anthem is being played. And while such a lapse is not to be excused, it is far less serious than desecrating the flag publicly or attempting to create a disturbance during the playing of the national anthem so that no one else may honor it.

Just so with the priests; it might have been possible that a prophet would observe in them some oversight in the carrying out of their duties, forgetting to do this or that religious custom. But these priests were despising the whole business in which they were engaged and the profession to which they had been called. And that is what could not be overlooked. Consequently, Malachi returned to this theme a few verses later because of its gravity.

2. Acceptable offerings (1:7–9)

In close conjunction with his opening salvo, Malachi moves from a general accusation to the description of a specific failure of the priests. "You place defiled food on my altar," God said to them (v. 7), and such a charge was very serious indeed. The biblical manual for the practice of the priesthood was Leviticus. Even a cursory reading of this book reveals a passion for purity and cleanliness in every area of life; but especially in regard to worship. Cleanliness was absolutely essential. Two particular statements from Leviticus indicate this concern clearly. In 22:2 Moses is commanded by Yahweh to order the priests "to treat with respect the sacred offerings." In 22:9 Yahweh decrees that "the priests are to keep my requirements so that they do not become guilty [better, "incur sin"] and die for treating them with contempt." Certainly nothing could be clearer than that the business of being a priest was intended to be taken as a serious occupation. The death penalty was prescribed for any priest who treated his duties lightly, and such contempt was equated with *sin*.

If Malachi was correct, if the priests really had despised God's name and had been involved with defiled food (used in offerings), they were living on borrowed time. Already the death penalty should have been meted out to them, according to the law of Moses, which they were sworn to uphold! It is only natural, therefore, that they should want to know how they had failed, though one gets the impression from

Malachi that their problem was not really ignorance of what they should or should not have been doing. Still, in response to the questions that Malachi attributed to them, an answer is given.

In simple terms the priests were bringing to Yahweh, their Father, gifts that no one would dare to present to the Persian governor living in Jerusalem at the time. Blind, crippled, or diseased animals offered to a human leader would have brought instant reprisal. It is no wonder that Malachi concluded that the choice of such poor beasts as offerings to Yahweh was a sign of contempt. Two times he asks rhetorically in paraphrase, "When you do things like this, is that not wrong?" And the word translated "wrong" is much stronger in Hebrew than the English word implies. It is the word *ra'*, which is normally translated "evil" throughout the Old Testament. Again, Malachi hammers home the point that the priests were not merely *incorrect* (as "wrong" would imply), but positively *evil* in the way they treated God. His conclusion, again using the device of a rhetorical question, is devastating: "With such offerings from your hands, will he [God] accept you?" (v. 9).

Some scholars make much of the fact that Malachi seems to be overly concerned with what may be called the ritual aspect of service to God. Indeed, many Christians might be tempted to feel that Malachi was making a big fuss over a small matter. After all, we do not offer animal sacrifices any more. But such an argument misses the entire thrust of Malachi's sermon. In *his* day the "how" of religious worship was believed to be important by everyone. One's carefulness in the details of offering sacrifices was a way of testifying to the significance that one's religion had in one's entire life. But beyond that, Malachi must be understood to be dealing here with a principle that is basic to any situation. It does matter how one worships God. Does singing that is purposely off-key show respect for God, or contempt? What would be the impact on a congregation whose minister would appear Sunday morning unshaven, shirtless, in baggy shorts, and wearing shower slippers! Could anyone really think a minister was serious about serving God if the sermon of the morning were less than half as interesting and much more poorly prepared than a speech delivered at a pep rally the night before? In short, the attitude one displays quite often says a great deal about the relative significance that one attaches to various parts of life. What Malachi was denouncing was not merely the way things were being done but the indifference to God that *caused* things to be done so poorly.

It is certainly true that the *way* in which things are done almost always will have a great impact on the relative *importance* that is attached to them. What Malachi was urging should surely be at least a minimum requirement for all spiritual service. One ought not offer to God anything one would be ashamed to offer to any human being.

3. *The real purpose of worship (1:10–11)*

In addition to what has been argued above, there is another side to the issue. Because of the necessary emphasis that was placed on the ways in which acceptable worship should be offered to God, one of the continual problems faced by the people of Israel in all generations was the temptation to believe that by *doing* what the law stipulated they were actually fulfilling the true *intention* of that law. It was precisely because of the persistence of this misconception that more than one Israelite prophet took the people to task for failing to remember that God was demanding *being* as well as *doing*. In fact, some of these prophets—such as Amos, Hosea, and Isaiah—had stated quite starkly that the doing of religious service had no value in and of itself. Notice, for example, these words of the LORD spoken by Amos:

> I hate, I despise your religious feasts; I cannot stand your assemblies. Even though you bring me burnt offerings and grain offerings, I will not accept them. Though you bring choice fellowship offerings, I will have no regard for them. Away with the noise of your songs! I will not listen to the music of your harps (Amos 5:21–24).

Isaiah, the younger contemporary of Amos, said virtually the same thing:

> "The multitude of your sacrifices—what are they to me?" says the Lord. "I have more than enough of burnt offerings, of rams and the fat of fattened animals; I have no pleasure in the blood of bulls and lambs and goats. When you come to meet with me, who has asked this of you, this trampling of my courts? Stop bringing meaningless offerings! Your incense is detestable to me. New Moons, Sabbaths and convocations—I cannot bear your evil assemblies. Your New Moon festivals and your appointed feasts my soul hates. They have become a burden to me; I am weary of bearing them. When you spread out your hands in prayer, I will hide my eyes from you; even if you offer many prayers, I will not listen" (Isa. 1:11–15).

What was the reason for God's displeasure? "Your hands are full of blood," is the reason Isaiah gave (1:15). And in the words of God quoted by Hosea, "I desire mercy, not sacrifice, and acknowledgment of God rather than burnt offerings" (6:6). Many other writers made the same or a similar point. Only persons with "clean hands and a pure heart" could hope to stand in the presence of God (Ps. 24:4), and no one could possibly be rendered clean as long as a life style of rebellion against the ethical demands of God was practiced. As Amos stated, "Let justice roll on like a river, righteousness like a never-failing stream!" (5:24). Persons who cheated their neighbors during the week could not enter the sanctuary on the Sabbath and expect that merely by offering a sacrifice or by bringing some money they could placate God. Rather, in the penetrating words of Isaiah once again, they should "stop doing wrong" and "learn to do right" (1:16–17).

Malachi, therefore, stands within a great tradition when he expresses God's wish that someone would lock the temple doors to prevent the continuation of worship that was simply useless. The important point is this. In no case will *offerings* be pleasing or acceptable to God if they come from *people* who are displeasing to Him. Notice what Yahweh says in verse 10: "I am not pleased with *you* [!] . . . and I will accept no *offering* from your hands."

There is just reason for Yahweh's discontentment. While His own priests dishonored Him, defiling and mocking the entire process of worshiping Him, His reputation outside Israel was growing. The name (reputation) of Yahweh was "great" (famous) throughout the known world according to verse 11. Note that the future tense of the NIV "My name will be great" is unwarranted. The Hebrew text is more accurately translated by the present tense as in RSV and JB): "My name is great." Indeed, "pure offerings" were made to Yahweh throughout the world because of His surpassing greatness; but in Yahweh's own land, the home that He had given as a covenantal gift to His people, priests continued useless and insulting worship practices because they did not respect God enough to worship Him properly. Here is the final pillar in Malachi's argument for the true purpose of careful worship. God is great. He deserves the best that human beings can offer. His greatness warrants the finest of which they are capable in every respect. What better reason than this is there for us to take seriously the business of worship? God is great. In the argument of Malachi, that says it all.

4. *Once again, the matter of acceptability (1:12–14)*

Malachi now returns to the theme of verses 7–9. Very little new is contained in this section. Additional illustrations are offered concerning the shortcomings of the priests. Verse 12 portrays them once again as profaning God's name (see v. 7). But this time their attitude of contempt is described in full color. Malachi accuses the priests of saying that their Deity's table (place of sacrifice) and the food (animal contents used in offerings) were defiled and contemptible respectively. Now, as noted in the Introduction, no priest would actually have said such things out loud, even if he believed they were true. But Malachi was basing his interpretation on solid footing. Watching them "sniff . . . contemptuously" while carrying out their duties, observing that their profession was viewed more as a burden than a holy privilege, what else could he conclude? Malachi seemed to know, even in his day, that "actions speak louder than words."

Once again, therefore, Malachi reminds the priests that God is not fooled by them. They may continue to use injured, crippled, and diseased animals, but this did not mean that God would accept them or that He would view the responsibilities of the priests as having been carried out properly. Instead, the persons who persisted in such mockery would be in for a real shock. God would curse them!

At this point Malachi begins to tie together the various strands of his argument. In verse 14 the three major ideas discussed in the preceding verses are all mentioned. First, acceptability must be understood. Animals fit for sacrifice to God could be located. God's requirements were not impossible to meet. Some people even owned an acceptable animal in their very own flocks. Knowing well the quality that would be required, they vowed to give their best animals to God. But because of their true feelings of boredom with and indifference to God they made a last-minute switch before worship time. In the end God received only another blemished animal. Well, precisely this type of person would be cursed, not because God was so strict but because what was acceptable was withheld from Him.

Second, the greatness of God is underscored. Because He is great, He has the sovereign freedom to curse those who despise Him. Repetition of the word *great* ties this final section of the paragraph not only to an earlier verse in the same sermon (see v. 11) but also to the first sermon in the book (see 1:5). In terms of style the word *great* is probably largely responsible for the juxtaposition of sermons one and two in this sequence. What the Edomites needed to learn (v. 5) the Israelite priests also had forgotten. Yahweh is great—great enough to accomplish whatever He desires. Now this great Yahweh had promised to bless those who obeyed Him but to curse those who did not (read

Deut. 30:11–19). Above all, religious professionals should have known His greatness.

Third, Malachi returns to the subject of respect, representing Yahweh as declaring that His name was feared (better translated "respected") among the nations (cf. 1:5 again). This is evidently Malachi's way of asserting that the greatness of Yahweh would normally produce respect. That it did not, even among the priests, was very surprising. Indeed, these priests who did not fear Yahweh could not graduate from the first grade. They did not even remember that "respect for Yahweh is where wisdom begins" (Prov. 1:7 CDI)!

B. The Importance of Faithfulness to an Original Calling (2:1–9)

1. Curse versus blessing (2:1–3)

Already in 1:14 Malachi had spoken of the possibility that Yahweh would curse anyone who insisted on offering animals that were less than the best he had. Again, in the present section, the subject of a divine curse is broached. Now, a curse in the Old Testament was not at all like a swear word or a vulgar epithet. In the context of the relationship between God and Israel a curse was a vital part of the covenant. That is, from the very beginning Israel had been given to understand that God's treatment of them would be conditional on their response to His moral demands. Always there had been strong emphasis on the positive aspect of the matter and a clear understanding that Israel could expect divine blessing if they obeyed their covenant partner. But also from the beginning there had been a strong emphasis given to the possibility that Israel might not obey. In such a case Israel was to expect a divine curse.

The important point to be remembered is that both the blessing and the curse were vital to the covenant relationship between Yahweh and Israel. Every contract written in the ancient Near Eastern world contained contingency clauses. If the parties involved fulfilled their respective obligations under the terms of the contract, well and good. If either did not, the curse clause of the contract was automatically to take effect. That is, the contract (covenant) was not made ineffective; but the negative aspect anticipated and provided for from the beginning was simply invoked.

Numerous examples in the Old Testament illustrate this dual aspect of the Israelite covenant with Yahweh. For example, Exodus 20:5–6 plainly stipulates that Israel may expect commandment breakers to be punished (v. 5), while at the same time promising that commandment keepers would be recipients of the faithful covenant love of God (v. 6). But by far the most striking example of this duality occurs in Deuteronomy. Chapter 28 preserves two rather ancient poems that dramatize the respective results of obedience and disobedience. They are given here in parallel columns so that their relationship to each other may be observed clearly.

You will be *blessed* in the city and *blessed* in the country.	You will be *cursed* in the city and *cursed* in the country.
The fruit of your womb will be *blessed*, and the crops of your land and the young of your livestock—the calves of your herds and the lambs of your flocks.	Your basket and your kneading trough will be *cursed*.
Your basket and your kneading trough will be *blessed*.	The fruit of your womb will be *cursed*, and the crops of your land, and the calves of your herds and the lambs of your flocks.
You will be *blessed* when you come in and *blessed* when you go out.	You will be *cursed* when you come in and *cursed* when you go out.
(Deut. 28:3–6)	(Deut. 28:16–19)

The significance of all this should not be missed. Under the terms of the covenant Yahweh had *obligated* Himself to respond to disobedience with curses! Blessing was not to be showered freely on persons who did not even attempt to honor their part of the deal. And that is just the point Malachi seems to be making in his sermon aimed at the priests. Unless they began immediately to listen to God and to honor His name (recall the use of the word *honor* in 1:6!), God would have no alternative but to reverse the blessings that they had come to take for granted.

Verse 3 serves as a concrete example of just how frightful it would be to live under a divine curse. The word translated "offal" by NIV is the Hebrew word used to refer to the entrails of an animal that has been sacrificed. One of the basic rules of offering a sacrifice properly, according to Leviticus, was that these entrails had to be taken to a location outside the camp and destroyed (see Lev. 4:11–12; 8:17; 16:27). Now the curse that Yahweh threatens to enact against the disobedient priests is that He will smear this gory offal on the faces of the priests. Not only was such an action intended to be humiliating, but it would also disqualify the priests involved from serving in the temple because of their uncleanness! Still there was more. With their faces smeared so horribly with repugnant entrails, the priests themselves would be carted bodily out of the camp to be isolated from the community of the people of God.

2. *The way it used to be (2:4-7)*

In these verses Malachi provides perhaps the loftiest statement of purpose regarding an ordained priesthood (ministry) to be found anywhere in Scripture. Nowhere else in the Old Testament—except in Numbers 25:12-13—is the ordination of the Levitical priests described as a covenant. In Malachi's thinking, their calling to specific religious duties warranted such a lofty designation, and Malachi defines his term well enough to avoid the possibility of misunderstanding. In short, the arrangement between Yahweh and Levi was as follows. To the priests Yahweh promised life and peace. In exchange, the priests were expected to offer Yahweh reverence (v. 5). Further, on condition of proper service to Yahweh, the priests would have occasion to remember a very ancient promise that had been pronounced on them—a covenant in which Yahweh had been called on to bless their skillful work and to show pleasure at their performance (Deut. 33:11).

Verse six is the key to this Malachian perception of the true function of a minister of God. Such persons obviously should *speak* correctly ("True instruction was in his mouth and nothing false was found on his lips") and *live* correctly ("He walked with me in peace and uprightness"). But their responsibilities do not end there. They should also exert a positive, converting influence on others ("[he] turned many from sin")! By telling his audience that the priests had done precisely these things in the early years of the Levitical priesthood, Malachi underscores his belief that this good start should have been continued without interruption. "The lips of a priest ought to preserve knowledge, and from his mouth [people] should seek instruction" (v. 7). That is, had the priests continued faithfully to perform up to the standards originally set forth for them, people could have continued to seek truth and redeeming knowledge from them. Unfortunately, however, Malachi can no longer use a simple declarative sentence to describe the actual conduct of the priests. He turns instead to a conditional *ought* and an obligatory *should* in sad testimony to the fact that Levi's sons no longer could be counted on to do their job within the covenant community. They used to do it, Malachi is saying, and they ought to be doing it still, but they have failed sadly.

It is of utmost significance that Malachi does not repeat here the charge of laxity in matters of ritual observance and detail. He zeroes in instead on the teaching ministry as the most significant area of priestly responsibility. The true instruction on which earlier generations had been able to depend should have been inherited by the current generation of Israelites in the forms of knowledge and of instruction. Instruction in moral and spiritual matters was vital to the continued health of the people of God. Sons and daughters must have the opportunity to discover the meaning of their parents' faith if ever these children are to make it their own (see Deut. 6:6-9, 20-24). The group charged with the responsibility of this education was the company of priests, in the view of Malachi. A priest was to be, in fact, a "messenger of the LORD Almighty" (Mal. 2:7)!

3. The way it is (2:8-9)

These verses, standing immediately following Malachi's exalted perception of what a priest *should* be, serve a shocking function. The priests (ministers), who were expected to turn people from sin (v. 6), have themselves turned aside from the way of God (v. 8). Those whose teaching should have been the epitome of truth, which establishes moral uprightness (v. 6), instead espoused teaching that caused people to stumble (v. 8). Little wonder that Malachi concludes, "You have violated the covenant" (v. 8). Indeed, they had turned it upside down! Everything that should have been turned *away from* they had turned *toward*. That which should have produced *sure footing* they had turned into *stumbling blocks*.

Again, in accordance with the stipulations of a legal contract, God is portrayed by Malachi as being left with no choice. Those who had despised God would come to be despised by the very people they were supposed to serve. Those who had treated God with contempt and disrespect would be humiliated before all the people. In short, the reward these priests would get would be justly deserved, for exactly what they had done to God would be done to them. They had sown the wind. They would reap the whirlwind! They should not have deceived themselves, for "God cannot be mocked" (Gal. 6:7).

For Further Study

1. How much honor do we give to God if a medical doctor is required to study for ten years or more but we allow a person to teach Scripture or preach with no requirement for study and learning? Should there be an educational minimum for all ministers? Should there be any kinds of requirements for ministers?

2. How important is the form of worship that is followed from week to week in the church or the synagogue that you attend?

3. How does one resolve the natural tension between form and formality, between required procedures in worship and merely perfunctory responses to God?

4. Would you call the elevated social status of the priests in ancient Israel a privilege? What would Malachi have called it?

5. This sermon in Malachi is addressed to religious professionals. Does it have any relevance for lay persons?

Chapter 5

A Community in Covenant
(Malachi 2:10–16)

In terms of the structure posited for each sermon in the Introduction, this oracle presents a few difficulties at first glance. The "Strong Statement" is clearly made in v. 11 ("Judah has broken faith") and there is an "Anticipated Question" in verse 14 ("Why?"), though this question is really in response to the second accusation ("Another thing you do . . .") made by the prophet in verse 13. The separation of an "Elaboration" within the tiny paragraph is difficult unless one views virtually everything except the strong statement and the anticipated question as being elaboration. These stylistic peculiarities notwithstanding, the meaning of the paragraph is rather straightforward.

A. Breaking Faith

Verses 11–16 exhibit what scholars commonly refer to as an "envelope structure." That is, the thought that begins verse 11 is the same as the one that ends verse 16 (breaking faith), and these two points normally signal the limits of a unit of thought or of speech in the Old Testament. Leaving aside a discussion of verse 10 for the moment, and assuming that verses 11–16 are, in fact, a unit more or less tightly constructed around the idea of breaking faith, it becomes possible for us to delve into the meaning of the argument being presented.

The problem is stated at the beginning of the paragraph in simple terms: "Judah has broken faith" (v. 11); then the solution is given at the end of the paragraph: "Do not break faith" (v. 16). However, the argument is not quite so simple as such a formulation might appear to make it. The verb that is translated "break faith" occurs four times in verses 11–16. This frequency of occurrence alone makes it likely that we have to do here with a *key word* for the paragraph, an assumption that is borne out upon further examination.

The verb translated "break faith" is derived from a common noun in Hebrew, the noun translated "garment." Although no connection is apparent between this verb and this noun in English, the verb translated "break faith" is related closely to the noun translated "garment" in Hebrew. In Hebrew, a garment *(beged)* is the simplest, plainest piece of outer clothing in a wardrobe. That means, among other things, that everyone, no matter how poor, would own at least a *beged*, in addition to some kind of undergarment that one could acceptably use in everyday work. Now people poor enough to afford only a *beged* would use their single garment for more reasons than clothing themselves during the day. Typically, they would use it as bedding during the night, too. The same piece of clothing thus had a dual function for poor people. Because of this, the legal codes of ancient Israel provided that a garment could be used as collateral for a loan but that it could not be retained by the creditor overnight. The reason was obvious. Persons who were so poor as to be able to secure a loan with nothing other than the only piece of clothing they owned should not be maltreated. Especially forbidden was the taking of a widow's *beged* as pledge for a loan (see Deut. 24:17).

What the Hebrews did with the noun *beged* was to revocalize it as if it were a verb, *bagad*. As a verb, it originally meant the improper taking of a *beged* but it soon came to describe other acts that were improper within the setting of a community supposedly composed of equal partners in covenant with God. Cheating, swindling the gullible, defrauding poor or helpless members of society, etc.—all were called *beged*-ing or "garmenting." And since this cheating or defrauding was taking place within the confines of a religious community, it is quite proper to translate the verb (with NIV) as "break faith."

To repeat, this verb translated "break faith" is the key to the entire paragraph. As noted earlier, it begins and ends the sermon (vv. 11, 16), and it is commonly recognized that the specific act of faith breaking scored here by the prophet is related to the sphere of marriage. Thus, verse 11 defines the treachery of Judah—the detestable thing that was being committed—as being a desecration of the Lord's beloved sanctuary by means of marrying "the daughter of a foreign god." Now, marriage to foreign wives, while known in early Israelite history, should have been recognized for what resulted from it. Such mixed marriages almost invariably produced friction of one kind or another; for sooner of later the foreign women desired to import their own native gods into Israel for worship. And though we do not condone the worship of foreign gods as a correct practice theologically, one cannot deny the fact that people should expect to be given freedom to worship the deities of their parents and their homeland. The trouble in Israel came when these foreign religions became attractive to Israelites who should have been as devoted to Yahweh as the foreigners were to the false gods of their respective nations.

Many examples of the troubles that all too frequently arose out of a mixed marriage situation may be cited. In Numbers 12 the Cushite wife of Moses became the object of rather intense jealousy on the part of Miriam and Aaron (Moses' sister and brother). Finally, a situation developed that can only be described as crisic in proportion (see especially vv. 10–13). The point here is that even divine vindication of the choice of a foreign wife in the particular case of Moses (see vv. 6–8) did not prevent trouble among the members of the group who were attempting to cause trouble for Moses as their leader.

A second kind of difficulty that developed because of mixed marriages is exemplified by the experiences of two kings. Solomon, with all the promise of his lineage and great heritage, still fell prey to this disease. "As Solomon grew old, his wives turned his heart after other gods, and his heart was not fully devoted to the Lord his God, as the heart of David his father had been" (1 Kings 11:4). And Ahab, given credit for little that was positive in his reign by the prophetic interpreters of his career, was remembered as the one who had imported Baal worship into Israel under the influence of his Baal-worshiping wife, Jezebel. This is the commentary on his career: "Ahab son of Omri did more evil in the eyes of the Lord than any of those before him" (1 Kings 16:30).

With examples like these and many others that could be recalled— examples that came from Israel's history—surely the people who lived in the time of Malachi should have realized the potential for trouble that inheres in a mixed marriage. Here it should be emphasized that by mixed marriage the biblical writer did not mean a mixture of racial types, social strata, or economic levels. He meant, purely and simply, a marriage between a believer in Yahweh, the God of Israel, and an unbeliever. This rejection of religiously mixed marriages was judged to be correct by mainstream Christianity, as may be noted in the following extended quotation of Paul.

Do not be yoked together with unbelievers. For what do righteousness and wickedness have in common? Or what fellowship can light have with darkness? What harmony is there between Christ and Belial? What does a believer have in common with an unbeliever? What agreement is there between the temple of God and idols? For we are the temple of the living God. As God has said: "I will live with them and walk among them, and I will be their God, and they will be my people."

"Therefore come out from them
and be separate,

says the Lord.

Touch no unclean thing,
and I will receive you."
"I will be a Father to you,
and you will be my sons and daughters,

says the Lord Almighty."
(2 Cor. 6:14–18)

Two things must be noted about this view presented by Paul in this passage. First, he was most probably addressing persons who were still single, giving advice to young people about how to plan for a believer's marriage. Second, in these five verses Paul refers to statements made in the Old Testament books of Leviticus, Ezekiel, Jeremiah, Isaiah, and Hosea! This he did, no doubt, to emphasize the fact that his was no new argument but an honored and traditional one. To those whom Paul might have cited to further support his argument, Malachi certainly could have been added.

B. The Covenant of Marriage

Verse 14 firmly asserts that God serves as a witness to the legal contract (covenant) of marriage. In fact, Proverbs 2:17 explicitly describes marriage as a *divine* covenant! That is why Malachi is so concerned about the dissolving of marriage; it is an example of breaking faith among his people. Unfaithfulness in marriage is tantamount to unfaithfulness to God Himself. This is just another example of what happened in Israel when the people forgot their history and the promises they had made to God. Not only were they intermarrying with pagan foreigners, but they were also divorcing their godly Israelite wives to be free to do so. The prophet gives three reasons why this practice is wrong.

First, it is wrong to divorce the wife of one's youth because it involves breaking faith with her. As a partner to the marriage, she too had been involved in a *triangle relationship* of man, woman, and God. Not only was there a sin against God, as seen above, but there was also a sin against one of God's children, the faithful wife who had loved her husband for many years. It is of extreme importance to notice here that *no* cause is advanced against these faithful partners. They are simply flung aside in favor of the devotees of pagan gods. It is little wonder that Malachi declares that men who act this way must be excommunicated (v. 12). Nor should anyone be surprised that God refuses to hear the prayers or accept the offerings of such men (v. 13).

There is a second reason why it is wrong to divorce a godly woman to marry an ungodly one. Religious intermarriage blocks one of the highest goals of God for the people who serve Him. Verse 15 informs the readers that God creates and sustains two of His children together in the marriage union for the holy purpose of producing godly offspring. According to Malachi's reasoning, if God is partner to and witness of a marriage and blesses the bond between two of His children, any children they produce belong to Him. That is, they belong to Him just as their parents belong to Him. This is one important way in which the holy family of God is enlarged.

Malachi surely was giving the ancient Israelites such instructions pertaining to marriage for a good reason—their children. In a marriage between one person devoted to Yahweh and another person devoted to Baal (or Marduk or Re or any other deity), to whom do the children belong? There is no such creature as a "half-Yahwist" (or a half-Christian!). That is why God refuses to bless or sanction unions in which Christians marry unbelievers. Such unions do not generally produce the kind of offspring He seeks: children belonging from birth exclusively to Him. Yet even in marriages in which one partner becomes a Christian, God does have a special claim on the children (cf. 1 Cor. 7:12–14).

It need not be assumed from Malachi's argument that godly parents always produce godly children. What Malachi means is that it is natural for this to be the case. Each child will soon come to assert his or her own will in the matter of serving God. This fact always implies the freedom to choose *not* to be a godly offspring. And the opposite may also be ture, of course, for the children of unbelieving parents may decide for God on their own. But if the argument of Malachi is to be taken seriously, what is clear is that such cases are unnatural and unlikely. Children do tend to serve the God of their parents!

Malachi's third reason against divorce and remarriage to an unbeliever is given in verse 16: "I hate divorce." This statement must not be taken out of its proper context. True, God is being quoted here by the prophet. True, a straightforward statement is being made. But it is also true that the kind of divorce under discussion is clearly defined as "a man's covering himself with violence." Divorce between two believers is the issue, and the believer's divorcing of his wife is called violence. With these limitations this statement stands as the strongest and most explicit Old Testament expression on the subject of marriage and divorce. Israelites of Malachi's day were admonished to "guard" themselves and were sternly commanded, "Do not break faith" (v. 16). To divorce a godly woman was to engage in a practice that God Himself hates. And since serious problems demand stern and disciplined solutions, Malachi here couches his commandment in the grammatical form used in the Ten Commandments. Even as the seventh commandment reads, "Never commit adultery" (for such is the force of the Hebrew construction in Exodus 20:14), so Malachi now admonishes, "Never break faith" (using exactly the same construction!). The best way to "guard yourself in your spirit" (Mal. 2:16) (this phrase simply means to be extremely cautious) is to set your mind so firmly on *faithfulness* that you will simply refuse to allow the thought of the possibility of *un*faithfulness to enter your mind. Just as you would never murder, steal, lie on the witness stand, or covet, so Malachi boldly asserts that you must never be unfaithful!

C. The Involvement of the Community (2:10)

There are good reasons for having reserved comment on verse 10 until now. As argued above, the real meat of the paragraph is delineated by the opening and the closing words in verses 11 and 16 respectively. And, as also was made clear above, the specific example of faith breaking cited by Malachi concerned divorce and remarriage to unbelievers. Verse 10 both does and does not fit within this specific context. Although it does contain the words *breaking faith*, it is not concerned so much with any *particular* example as with the *general* principle of keeping faith within a covenantal society or community. It is entirely possible that Malachi may have uttered what now appears as verse 10 in connection with a sermon other than the one that now follows in verses 11–16. That would mean that his editor (discussed in chapter 1) could have placed verse 10 here between the sermon against the priests and the one on divorce.

At any rate, there are adequate reasons for the placement of verse 10 in its present position. First, as we have noted, verse 10 is not concerned with divorce but with the general principle of breaking faith. Notice that the question of the prophet is concerned with his people's breaking faith with one another. Now, this phrase "one another" has an interesting history and function in biblical Hebrew. Literally, the entire question reads, "Why are we breaking faith, each one with his brother?" And the word *brother* does not mean a blood relative but a person of more or less equal social, community, and religious status. Malachi is asking why Israelite is breaking faith with Israelite, child of God cheating (defrauding, abusing, etc.) child of God. He continues his thought by defining such activity as a profaning of the covenant of their fathers.

Second, if this general accusation of the prophet is to have an effect on his audience, at least one specific illustration must be used. Marriage is a natural illustration. The family-oriented language of verse 10 (fathers, brother) is expanded to include daughter (of a foreign god in verse 11) and children (in the phrase "godly offspring," verse 15). The breaking of faith is pointedly specified, and the general rule of verse 10 is borne out by the specific example in verses 11–16.

Third, the concept of a covenant that refers in verse 10 to the entirety of the traditional faith of Israel is focused in verses 11–16 on one very limited kind of legal transaction, or covenant.

We may now return to a close examination of verse 10. Really, there are two concepts presented in the verse, and these serve as antitheses of each other. The first is the idea of the fatherhood of God. As noted in the commentary on the first chapter of Malachi, Israel enjoyed thinking of herself as the child of God. And here the prophet affirms the basic truth of such a belief. Every member of the community in ancient Israel was truly a child of God since He had made a special covenant with Israel. But "like priest, like people" is the sad commentary that Malachi makes on those hearing him. Even as the priests consistently failed to give God the honor due to any father (1:6), so also the people failed to act as proper children would to their father. And their offense against God was that they were breaking faith with each other! The words of John restate this basic principle in unequivocal terms: "If anyone says, 'I love God,' yet hates his brother, he is a liar. For anyone who does not love his brother, whom he has seen, cannot love God, whom he has not seen" (1 John 4:20).

The second concept, the idea of genuine brotherhood, therefore, flows naturally out of the first concept of fatherhood. Recall once again that a brother in these contexts means an equal. Thus, verse 10 introduces what will be an absolutely stunning idea in the sermon on divorce to follow. One of the most dastardly ways in which Israelites were breaking faith with their *equals* was by dealing unfairly with their *wives!* Wives, too, could lay claim to God as their Father. Women, too, were partners in the covenant (note verse 14: "she is your partner"). How absurd it was for men who claimed to be the sons of God to break faith with one who was a covenant *partner* and *equal* in order to become involved with one who was the "daughter" of another "father"!

The plea of the prophet now stands in bold relief against the backdrop of his perception of the way a real family of God ought to function. Each member of the family, male and female, should claim and hallow the privilege of being a child of God. This places God, as Father, at the top of the family. He is in charge. He controls. He sets the rules. And His children keep faith with *Him* by keeping faith with *each other*. They must honor their covenant with Him by sticking to covenants made between themselves. They must maintain a pure, spiritual heritage by avoiding marital involvement with those who do not have God as their Father. And they must produce godly children, who will repeat in their lives the kind of faithfulness modeled for and bequeathed to them by their parents.

For Further Study

1. Read an article on marriage in one of the Bible dictionaries or encyclopedias listed in the bibliography. Was Malachi's view of marriage fairly consistent with other biblical passages on the subject?

2. Evidently, Malachi had a very high conception of the significance and worth of a woman in the marital union. Do you think he would accept the view that the woman must play an inferior role to the man in marriage? In what sense do you think Malachi believed a woman to be the equal of a man?

3. Do you like the phrase "family of God"? What does it mean to you?

4. Should a Christian marry a non-Christian today? Why, or why not?

5. Is this sermon by Malachi really about divorce as we generally use the term now?

Chapter 6

The Problem of God's Justice
(Malachi 2:17–3:5)

Strong Statement: "You have wearied the Lord with your words" (2:17a).

Anticipated Question: "How have we wearied him?" (2:17b).

Elaboration: The question of the justice of God can be solved properly only by a divine visit to His people.

In this paragraph the fatigue of God is traced to the incessant griping of the people. Their position was that the injustice or unfairness of God could be deduced by observation of the facts of life around them. Operating on the assumption that the pleasure of God could be discerned from certain external criteria, these people concluded that evildoers were more pleasing to God than others because the evildoers were prosperous in material ways. The answer of the prophet lies in his awareness that the justice of God must be viewed on a scale that is broader than simply the material aspect of life.

A. The Weariness of God (2:17)

The Hebrew word translated "wearied" in this verse is quite significant. Commonly the word was used to express the idea of someone's becoming physically tired because of hard labor (see Josh. 24:13; 2 Sam. 23:10; Prov. 23:4). But here and in Isaiah 43 a rather startling use is made of the word by applying the concept of fatigue (becoming tired, making weary, etc.) to God and to His people. For example, in Isaiah 43:22 Yahweh reminds the people of Israel that they have not made themselves tired on His account, meaning that they have not been very diligent in worship. In the very next verse (23) the people

are reminded that the demands that have been placed on them have
not been inordinate:

> I have not burdened you with grain offerings
> nor *wearied* you with demands for incense"

In fact, the very opposite was true, for verse 24 uses the same two
verbs (burdened, wearied) to show the shocking truth of the matter:

> "You have burdened me with your sins
> and *wearied* me with your offenses."

By placing these two verses together, the prophet has made an absolutely shocking point: "I have not . . . *wearied* you," but you have . . .
wearied me." And the Isaian judgment on the people was that their
sins and offenses constituted a wearisome burden for God.

In Malachi 2:17 the same accusation is made of the people. But this
time they weary God with their words. And as the prophet hastens to
explain, words such as the ones uttered by his audience weary God as
surely as did the outright sins of which Isaiah spoke. Even though the
people might pretend to be shocked at the very idea that their conver-
sations could offend God, the prophet was no less certain of his ground.
In short, his argument ran that God was getting tired of hearing people
raise doubts about His fairness. The taunting statement, "All who do
evil are good in the eyes of the Lord, and he is pleased with them," was
probably never made exactly that way by anyone. But the sentiment
was there, according to the prophet; it was proved in the way the
people lived. When people break God's rules, live carelessly, and
ignore the responsibilities of covenant relationships, they are saying by
their lives that they do not believe in the justice of God. And their
asking with mock sincerity, "Where is the God of justice?" is a certain
sign that the people really think God doesn't care, that He really is
absent, and that it makes no difference whether they live well or
carelessly. It is little wonder that words like these, "spoken" by their
lives, actually made God tired. (Recall here the relation between the
words *word* and *deed* in Hebrew thought, as explained in chapter 2.)

B. The Messenger and the Audience (3:1–4)
1. *The identity of the messenger (3:1)*

In real-life terms the prophet speaks for God, who answers the
criticism of the people. It has commonly been assumed that two different persons are described in 3:1: a messenger and the Lord. However,

the poetic structure of the verse points to another interpretation.
Notice the three lines of the poem:

> See, I will send *my messenger*, who will prepare
>   the way before me.
> Then suddenly *the [lord]* you are seeking will come
>   to his temple;
> the *messenger of the covenant*, whom you desire,
>   will come.

And notice also that all three lines, referring twice to a messenger and
once to the "lord," are given as direct speech from the LORD Almighty.
That is, the LORD (capital *L*) utters the poem as a whole in which
reference is made to a messenger (Malachi) and to a lord (small *l*).
There is, in fact, a third identification of the coming one as the covenantal messenger. All are announced by God as soon to appear in
answer to the complaints of the people about His justice. The simplest
way to understand a poem framed in this way is to assume that God is
referring to a single being by three different titles (my messenger, lord,
and a covenantal messenger). The word *lord* here is not the Hebrew
proper name *Yahweh* discussed in chapter 1. It is merely a common
noun referring to a person of noble station socially.

Before continuing, let us observe that early interpreters of the Book
of Malachi had some difficulty with this verse. As may be noted in the
final paragraph (4:5–6), the messenger of 3:1 is equated with Elijah.
And while Mark 9:11–13 appears to support such an equation, Mark
1:2–4 just as clearly identifies the unnamed messenger as John the
Baptist. Accordingly, most New Testament interpreters have viewed
the statement of Jesus ("Elijah has come") in Mark 9:13 as being in
harmony with Mark 1:2–4. The point that should be stressed here with
respect to the original statement of Malachi is that whoever the messenger was, he was to accomplish the purpose of God by addressing the
question of God's justice in a satisfactory fashion.

2. *The work of the messenger of the covenant (3:2–4)*

In spite of their loud protestations to the contrary, the people really
did not want to learn the truth about God. This prophet shows by
stating that no one would be able to survive God's coming to be present
among His people through the messenger of the covenant. The words
endure and *stand* both mean the same thing. When the village tough
snarls out his challenge, "I can lick any man in the place," every person
in a crowded room remains silently in his seat, and no one perseveres

in resisting him. Just so, when the messenger of the covenant appears, no one will be bold enough to stand and challenge him or persistently resist him.

And for good reason. This messenger would become involved in the work of cleansing and purifying. The refiner's fire is easily distinguishable. But the phrase *"launderer's soap"* is somewhat misleading. Professional garment cleaners are intended, to be sure, but they were not merely persons who ran a cleaning service for a living. Rather, people using this kind of soap were aiming at ritual cleanliness (see Jeremiah 2:22, in which is the only other Old Testament use of the word). This kind of soap produced garments such as those worn by the transfigured Jesus, as described in Mark 9:3. And as a refiner or a purifier the messenger would produce the kind of purification that would render people as well as garments clean enough to become involved in the service of God. That is why the sons of Levi, the priests, are the ones who must receive the cleansing. Only after enduring such a process would they be fit to make proper offerings to God—offerings that would be made in righteousness. And only such offerings would be acceptable to the Lord (Mal. 3:3–4).

Verses 2–4 thus point to the real problem. It was not the justice of God that needed to be investigated but the impurity of the people that needed to be cleansed. And it must be noted that the purity of the people, both priests and offerers, is linked closely with the early days of Israel's covenant with the Lord. Those "days gone by" or "former years" had witnessed a pure priesthood offering righteous service to God. And those days had also marked an era of God's acceptance of and pleasure with Israel. Now the circle has been drawn back to its beginning. God is *not* pleased with evildoers, as some claimed (2:17). Only pure and righteous priests and people please Him; only such are acceptable to Him (3:4). This was the real truth about God.

3. *A prophetic definition of justice (3:5)*

As is so often true in the prophetic literature, the view held by one of the prophets of God is just the opposite of that accepted widely among the people. This final verse of the sermon illustrates how differently Malachi viewed justice from most of the people. As shown earlier, the question being raised about the justice of God had finally made Him tired (weary). Now, after his description of the work of the Messenger of the covenant, Malachi moves to his own view of what real justice is.

In 3:5 he quotes the Lord Almighty once again (see 3:1) with the following points of emphasis.

First, God Himself would draw near for judgment or for *justice* (the same word in Hebrew as the final word in 2:17). And now, at last, the question "Where is the God of justice?" would be answered. He is drawing perilously near. And His near presence would be the guarantee of everything the people had pretended to desire, for God would serve as a speedy Witness ("I will be quick to testify").

Now Israelite tradition contained the recollection that on previous occasions God had been invoked as a witness in cases concerning His people. For example, Samuel had argued regarding his honesty as a public official by affirming, "The Lord is witness . . . that you have not found anything in my hand" (1 Sam. 12:5). And Job's reply to the taunts of his "friends" was simply that God would be his Witness (16:19) to the effect that he had lived a proper and a pure life. (See also Jer. 42:1–6). Thus, the people listening to Malachi would have known that more than one righteous and faithful person had turned finally to God for vindication of his life and service. Such memory should have been a source of assurance to them. But, as Malachi knew, his audience included no one in the class of a Samuel or a Job.

Thus, Malachi's second point about the kind of justice that God would enforce is made. The speediness of the trial promised by God would be of little comfort to those who were guilty of gross injustice. The prophet now specifies the kinds of things about which God declared Himself to be concerned.

The tables were turned once again. Whereas the people had complained that God was pleased with evildoers (2:17), the real truth was that God would be the first to take the stand against those who broke His covenantal standards. Notice the list of sins mentioned by Malachi. All of them relate to the practice of social injustice by people who exploited someone else merely because they had the power to do it.

Malachi warms to the task. He does not discuss the *legality* of the matter. He is concerned with the *justice* of it all. That is, he knows well enough that a rich and powerful exploiter might easily wave a legal document in the face of a weaker opponent. Probably the prophet himself had seen more than one home lost, more than one field change hands, more than one debt go unpaid—all because someone was powerful enough to "turn justice into bitterness" (Amos 5:7). Perhaps he even remembered the case of a queen who organized a totally "legal" transfer of the field of Naboth to the royal holdings simply by writing letters on the king's stationery ordering two witnesses to lie in court (see 1 Kings 21:1–16). So Malachi zeroes in on an issue that is higher in importance than mere legality. God would become involved personally in the defense of those who were too weak to defend themselves—widows, orphans, outsiders, and others who were vulnerable to oppression and cheating.

Malachi's point is clear. The very ones who were crying foul in 2:17 and demanding that God give an accounting of Himself and His justice were guilty of every crime in the book! In fact, they were even so bold as to accuse God of the very thing they were doing. But the prophet was not fooled. He equates this failure to deal fairly with the poor and the weak with failure to respect the God Whose justice was questioned in 2:17. And this, he argued, would all come to light in the presence of the God whom they had challenged. They had asked about justice, and justice they would get. God's justice. Justice for everyone. Justice even for those who were too oppressed and beaten down to speak for themselves. "Where is the God of justice?" He is going to take the witness stand to tell the real truth about the lives of His people. And the very evildoers who were supposed to be pleasing to Him would be the ones against whom His testimony would be given most forcibly. Who indeed would survive when He would draw near? He was "God of gods and Lord of lords, the great God, mighty and awesome, who shows no partiality and accepts no bribes. He defends the cause of the fatherless and the widow, and loves the alien, giving him food and clothing" (Deut. 10:17–18).

For Further Study

1. What is justice? What is the relationship between justice and legality?

2. Is injustice present in the church today? In the local congregation to which you belong? In the community that your church serves?

3. What would happen in your church next Sunday morning if God were to appear and agree to answer questions from the audience about His justice? What question would you ask? Do you think God would make any statements about the way things are done in your family? In your church? In your personal life?

4. Do you really want justice? Defend your answer.

Chapter 7

The Sins of Lay Persons
(Malachi 3:6–12)

Strong Statement: "You rob me [God]" (v. 8).

Anticipated Question: "How do we rob you?" (v. 8).

Elaboration: By failure to pay tithes and offerings, a lifestyle of disobedience is evident.

In this message Malachi illustrates the relationship between the failure of the people to obey God and the failure of God to bless them. God does not change in a capricious fashion from one moment to the next. If people change from obedience to disobedience, they must not expect God also to change the rules in order to accommodate them.

A. Returning to God (3:6–7)

The structure of these two verses has often been missed by translators. For example, note the rendition of NIV. But there is something very important being expressed in verse 6, namely the identity of the two parties who are to be involved in the sermon of the prophet. The first party is introduced by means of what scholars have called the self-revelation formula: "I am Yahweh." This phrase is the way in which the God of Israel introduces or expresses Himself to His people throughout the Book of Leviticus and in many other Old Testament passages. It is a common and well-known sentence. As a parallel to this identification of Yahweh, the second party is introduced in the same way, though in this case there is no other example of such an introduction of Israelites elsewhere in the Old Testament: "You are the sons of Jacob."

Given these two parties, a few words of description about each are added. The One who identifies Himself as Yahweh is also known as the Unchanging One. That is not to say that God is unchanging in the way that a stone or an inanimate object is unchanging. It is rather to assert that God is *dependable*. What He has been in the past is a clue to what He is now and also to what He will be in the future. It was considered quite important for Israel to know that her covenant Partner was not wishy-washy, that He could, in fact, be counted on whenever there was a crisis. The other party to the covenant, identified as the sons of Jacob, was also known as the indestructible one. That is not to say that Israel *could not* be destroyed but that she, in fact, *had not* been destroyed. Somehow, though this is not precisely clear, Malachi linked the survival of Israel (Jacob) with the dependability of God.

And this connection is an even greater mystery, given the history of Israel's covenant unfaithfulness. All the way back to the earliest patriarchs the characteristic trait of Israel had been noncompliance, failure to keep her part of the bargain with God, proclivity to turning away from the path marked so clearly by the rules accepted by both Israel and God as binding. So, to repeat, the very fact of the survival of Israel to that moment was remarkable. It was remarkable because God's grace, given all the credit in Romans 11:28–29, was remarkable beyond human imagination.

At this point Malachi becomes more than descriptive of what has been and presently still is happening between Israel and God. In the middle of verse 7 he moves to a prescription for the ills of his people. They must return to God, thus making it possible for God to return to them. Here it appears that in one sense both God and Israel had been changeless. God had not changed from His faithfulness, while Israel had not swerved from unfaithfulness expressed in various forms of disobedience. And given their past record of insensitivity to the demands of God, it is no wonder that the people questioned the prophet, "How are we to return?" And is it not apparent that even by asking the question in this way they were indicating the heart of their problem? They had existed so long in a state of turning away in the wrong direction that they could not imagine that they might need to face in the right direction and turn back (return) to God. And so, as he had done before (see chapter 4), Malachi moves from a general statement that contains a lofty standard to a specific example that illustrates the heart of that standard.

B. Keeping One of the Rules (3:8–11)

The way of returning to God begins by keeping His rules. Since tithing and the giving of offerings [anything set aside as a special gift for God, the priests, or the temple] were evidently among the best-known unkept rules to which Malachi could point, he asserts that his people needed to reapply these ancient rules to their lives before they could expect God to rain His blessings down on them.

This passage in Malachi raises a critical issue for interpreters. Malachi appears to be saying in a somewhat mechanical fashion that his audience could buy the blessing of God in exchange for their giving of tithes and offerings. Assuming this mechanical meaning for the words of the prophet, many commentators have rebuked Malachi for what they perceive to be a rather narrow point of view. Commonly they note that the earlier prophets all viewed rigorous ethical and moral demands as being the highest duty of people seeking favor from God. They reason, therefore, that at this point Malachi is really "less ethical and spiritual than . . . his great predecessors" (ICC, p. 72; see Bibliography).

Such a denunciation of Malachi seems hardly fair in the light of his messages regarding social and ethical standards elsewhere (as discussed in chapters 5 and 6, for example). And neither does it seem fair to Malachi for us to assume that he chose the issue of monetary gifts because it was the only thing that concerned him. Rather, exactly as he had done in his sermon regarding "a community in covenant" (chapter 5), he states a general principle to open his sermon (see v. 7) and proceeds to illustrate the truth of that general principle by means of a specific example. Again, it need not be assumed that there was only one answer that Malachi could have given to the self-righteous question of the people ("How are we to return?"). It is both simpler and more in keeping with his other preaching to assume that he used giving (not just tithing!) as only one example of many possible sins of which his people were guilty.

Other commentators, again assuming a mechanical sense as the only way to view the prophet's preaching, have elevated these particular words of Malachi to a place of prominence quite out of proportion to their function in the prophet's sermon. The ultimate extreme of this position results in citing these verses from Malachi to support a specific rule about tithing that a particular group desires to require of its members. Indeed, one may be denied a teaching or a preaching or a writing job with certain church groups if he is unwilling to agree that their interpretation of this verse represents the only biblical way for the work of God to be supported financially.

Now certainly any group has the right to set its own rules governing the ways in which its members will be required to support it. But as will be seen clearly below, there is no church or religious group in existence today that actually follows the biblical teaching on tithing. Those groups that claim they do so are merely deluding themselves and their followers. For while it may be admitted that the English word *tithe* is based on a Hebrew word that means a "tenth," there is other equally biblical information that few, if any, religious leaders wish to consider or to take literally.

In the first place, it should be noted that there are several different systems of tithing presented in various parts of the Old Testament. For example, we may observe the tithing rules presented in Deuteronomy 14:22–27. We should notice that an agricultural setting is assumed for the society that these rules address. We should notice also that this tithe was to be set aside during the time of harvest and saved back until it could be taken to the ". . . place the Lord your God will choose" (v. 25), where it was to be used in a meal of rejoicing over the blessings that God had bestowed. That is, ten percent of the produce (grain, new wine, oil, cattle, and sheep are mentioned in verses 22–23) was to be used to provide a special meal that the members of the household themselves would eat in celebration of God's goodness to them. The tithe was not given to the sanctuary but brought to the sanctuary so that the meal would include the Levites. Again, we must note the injunction to be joyous: "You and your household shall eat there in the presence of the Lord your God and rejoice" (v. 26!). It would appear clear, according to this passage, that this tithe belonged to the people whom God had blessed rather than to the "church" to which those people belonged.

Deuteronomy 14:28–29 takes the matter a step further. Every third year the members of individual households were not to use the tithe portion of their crops and flocks as a meal for themselves but were to set it aside in storage areas so that it could be used by the Levites (who were forbidden to grow their own crops), aliens (who might not have land on which to grow crops), the fatherless (whose parents were not alive to invite them to share in the produce of family farms), and widows (who traditionally have economic troubles in many societies).

This would mean either that one-third of the total tithe was to be set aside for such charitable purposes or that a second tithe was required. No one can be certain which of these two possibilities Deuteronomy 14 demanded.

Old Testament examples of tithe customs do not stop with this chapter in Deuteronomy. According to Numbers 18:21-32 the tithe was to be given to the Levites *every* year. An enigmatic story in Genesis 14 protrays Abraham paying tithe on the spoils of war to Melchizedek. A passage in Leviticus emphasizes the command to tithe everything produced from the soil as well as all animals born in one's flocks and herds (see Lev. 27:30-33); but there is no information given about what was to be done with this tithe—whether it was to be given to the sanctuary, eaten in celebrative joy by each family, reserved for Levites, or set aside for any poor person in the community is not stipulated. We are only reminded that the tithe belongs to Yahweh (verse 30), apparently upon the supposition that any of several valid uses could be made of it.

A second major point needs to be emphasized here. This variety of Old Testament views about tithing is not a negative sign but attests, rather, to the growth and vitality of the people of God engaged in a struggle to understand the issue over centuries of time. Economic systems based on agriculture naturally called for payment of tithes in produce. Later legislation provided for payment in silver. Generation after generation struggled with the issue, and the Bible has included as in some sense valid a variety of solutions. The important point is that there is no push within the biblical text itself to harmonize or to homogenize these different views of tithing into a single, universal rule that must be understood as legally binding on all people everywhere and in every circumstance. What should be noted, however, is this: Basic to all of the Old Testament passages that mention the tithe in one form or another is the theological assumption that God is the real Owner of everything that people "have." Tithing, however it was done, was merely human acknowledgment of the fact that people ought to stop and give thanks to God in some meaningful way for allowing them to enjoy *His* property for a while.

This brings us back to the issue of tithing in the time of Malachi. The plain truth is that we simply do not know to which particular tithing practice Malachi was referring, but obviously, his people knew what he meant. And whatever Old Testament tithing rules were currently in practice, both Malachi and the people knew that they were being neglected. Thus, his admonition relates to the people in their own circumstances, whatever they were and however strange they may seem to modern Americans. But we dare not forget that Malachi was arguing for a principle, not a specific interpretation of rules about tithing. This is made clear when Malachi begins to discuss his reasons for challenging people to practice a form of tithing (whatever form they knew and recognized to be valid for them). In essence Malachi mentions two things that go hand in hand. On the one hand, verse 7 contains the conditional promise that God would return to His children. On the other hand, verses 8–11 indicate what Israel must do to make His return to them a reality. By keeping God's rules properly, Israel could prove her good faith by a return to the old ways. And then God could begin to act in His old ways of blessing, too. Notice especially that there is no word given here about any kind of an automatic equation between the *amount* one gives and the *amount* of God's blessing. People who are rich cannot buy greater blessing from God simply by increasing their offering or tithe portion. The formula is far simpler than that. Put teeth to good intentions, act in concrete ways that God can see, and expect Him to act in His own beneficent way as well.

We should notice also the corporate nature of the promise. It was the entire nation that was languishing under a divine curse (3:9). Likewise, under the conditions explained above, the entire nation would once again witness the blessing of God. Crops would grow, pests would be thwarted, and the basis for a healthy farming economy would be reestablished. Malachi in this way reenforced the message of Deuteronomy: "So if you faithfully obey the commands I am giving to you today—to love the Lord your God and to serve him with all your heart and with all your soul—then I will send rain on your land in its season, both autumn and spring rains, so that you may gather in your grain, new wine and oil. I will provide grass in the fields for your cattle, and you will eat and be satisfied" (Deut. 11:13–15).

Perhaps a final word is in order. If, it may be asked, the traditional way of understanding tithing by many modern religious groups is set aside, how will the work of God be supported? The oft-neglected word of Malachi that follows the word *tithe* provides at least a partial answer. Notice that the robbery of God consisted not merely of the withholding of the tithe alone but also of the failure of the people to present offerings. Now the word *offerings* is used in as many different ways as the word *tithe*, just discussed. Some offerings were to be given in particular circumstances (such as in gratitude for a particular blessing from God), and other offerings were presented to God for other reasons (such as offerings made to atone for sin). But again, the basic principle on which the complex Old Testament view of offerings is founded is simple. The Israelites ought to realize that their Deity, who claimed them and made them His people, was worthy of receiving gifts. In this regard, it should be remembered that in addition to all the required offerings about which the Old Testament teaches, numerous passages assume that *freewill offerings* will be given by the people of God. These were voluntary and were to be given whenever a person wanted to give them.

In making a modern application of the Old Testament principles of giving to God and the church, perhaps the freewill offering provides the best point of application. Surely, persons who realize that their very existence is due to the good graces of God, who have been redeemed by His grace, and who understand that they are stewards always and owners never, will continue to support the work of God with greater generosity than *any* system could demand of them. Such persons will acknowledge that not only one-tenth but also the other ninety percent of what they enjoy belongs to God. In times of crisis they may respond to the needs of a church with gifts beyond the highest percentage any pastor would dream of fixing. In normal times they will give as much as they can in response to the needs of their church. And they, if Malachi was correct, will continue to know the blessings of God in ways that nongiving, self-oriented persons will never experience.

C. The True Purpose for God's Blessing (3:12)

This verse explains the real meaning of divine blessing and guards against misappropriation of the idea that God's blessing may be earned or bought by any means. Israel was to strive to receive the blessing of God not merely because the blessed life was satisfying and rewarding but chiefly because blessed people would function more appropriately as examples of the power of God to sustain those whom He had chosen to bear His name. Here Malachi returns to the theme that was expressed in 1:5 (see chapter 3). Among the prophets it was consistently believed and preached that Israel was destined to be a light to other nations, the means of salvation for non-Israelites. Malachi is true to this idea in the conclusion to this sermon when he argues that Israel ought to become a delightful land so that others would have the opportunity to observe the power of Israel's God (Yahweh) to bless His people. Thus, the real purpose for the reception of the blessing of God was to make Israel winsome enough, attractive enough, to other nations so that all people everywhere would be impelled to exclaim:

> Come, let us go up to the mountain of the Lord,
>   to the house of the God of Jacob.
> He will teach us his ways,
>   so that we may walk in his paths (Isa. 2:3).

For Further Study

2. What is your view of giving offerings (or even the tithe) to God? Is it possible for people to rob the church? God?

2. What is success? Is it different from prosperity? Are poor people ever successful?

3. What is the purpose of material prosperity? Are rich people less godly than others?

4. Read an article on tithing in one of the dictionaries listed in the bibliography. What is the contribution of Malachi to the subject?

Chapter 8

The Problem of Serving God
(Malachi 3:13–4:3)

Strong Statement: "You have said harsh things against me [God]" (3:13).

Anticipated Question: "What have we said against you?" (3:13).

Elaboration: It is not futile to serve God if the whole truth about His plan is understood.

In this sermon the prophet returns to his theme in the latter part of chapter 3. Those who conclude that serving God does not pay simply are not aware of the whole truth. They look only at the present, only at those who appear to prosper in material ways and who forget the future, at which time [God's time!] everything will finally be balanced properly.

A. Harsh Words for God (3:13–15)

Three different thoughts are expressed around the theme of harsh things being spoken against God (note again the use of the Hebrew word *davar*, which means either a "word" or a "thing" (cf. NIV). The first of these thoughts is the fact that the opening sentence of this sermon stands in precise parallel to the opening sentence of the fourth sermon of the prophet. "You have wearied the Lord with your words" (2:17), and "You have said harsh things against me" (3:13) mean exactly the same thing. Each statement introduces the people's problem with the fairness or the justice of God.

Second, the words of the people were considered harsh by the Lord because of their force. If what was being said by the Israelites were true, then the promise of 3:12 would be nullified. The people of Israel, who were known as those belonging to Yahweh, would not only be far less than winsome and attractive to the world but would, in fact, be repulsive. Who, indeed, would wish to serve a deity if nothing good were to be gained by it? Why would other nations come to Yahweh when His own people were filled with a sense of futility and despair in regard to their God? Such people would rather be stark testimony to the fact that the promised blessing sounded at the end of the preceding message was completely reversed.

Third, the harshness of what the people said lay in the fact that they were now guilty of the reversal of values of which they had accused God earlier. In 2:17, the first sermon on God's justice, they had accused God of taking delight in evildoers and of being pleased by them. In this sermon they themselves have been given over so completely to a sense of futility that *they* "call the arrogant blessed" (3:15). *They* conclude that evildoers prosper. *They*, in short, have reversed totally the proper scale of values honored by society. And the real tragedy of such a conclusion is that it was reached by "good" people. Notice that in the earlier sermon Malachi had severely reprimanded those who had phrased an improper accusation of God and had then revealed their own injustice and failure to revere God. In this sermon he does nothing similar. This can only be so because the misguided challengers of God of 3:13 were not guilty of the injustices named in 3:5. In one sense, however, for the good people, the ones still trying to follow God, to reach such a conclusion is even more damaging than for the obviously wicked to believe such falsehoods. If the righteous people had reached despair, where would any ray of hope begin?

B. God's Book (3:16)

Because Malachi did not need to reveal injustice in the lives of his audience in this sermon, he turned to another answer to questions about the fairness of God. God, he assured the audience, keeps a book, a "scroll of remembrance." He hears those who fear Him. He remembers their pain. He knows the anguish of their fears that life may not really be worth it all. And His way of working for good even with that which is apparently evil at the moment can be trusted even when it cannot be understood.

Malachi's reference to a scroll of remembrance would be particularly impressive to an audience living through an era of Persian control in their country. They would have known well that the practice of keeping records was a favorite custom of the Persian monarchs. They might even have known the story of Mordecai and King Xerxes as told in the Book of Esther. Mordecai had uncovered a plot by two men named Bigthana and Teresh to kill the king. When Mordecai had acted as a faithful citizen and had brought to the king's attention what was being plotted against him, Mordecai had received no reward whatsoever. But "all this was recorded in the book of the annals in the presence of the king" (Esth. 2:23). It was not until some time later that the king, unable to sleep, reviewed his book and was reminded of the faithfulness of Mordecai (6:1-2). Only then was Mordecai given proper honor and recognition (6:3).

The argument of Malachi seems to be that God would certainly do no less than a human emperor. Sooner or later, in His own time, God would "remember" the deeds of all His faithful servants. All who had served Him in any capacity would in due time receive their honor and recognition. That is, those who truly did fear God, who truly respected and served Him, were called to a lifestyle of hope. The *now* of God perhaps did not make proper sense. But the *future* of God would be far brighter than anyone could know. Those who "feared the Lord and honored his name" would not be forgotten. He would honor those who had honored Him.

C. God's Treasured Possession (3:17-18)

Malachi next turns to a different figure of speech to reemphasize his call to a lifestyle of hope. Again, the future tense is used: "They *will be* mine" (3:17) Now certainly those who have honored and served God should be thought of as belonging to Him every moment; God was not waiting until some future day to declare His acceptance of them. But there is another idea being stressed here—that the future holds the moment in which no one will be able to doubt in whose possession the faithful servants abide. No one who is wicked or dishonorable will be included as part of the "treasured possession" of God (v. 17). Everyone will know openly and without question who belongs to God. That is why the prophet can affirm in verse 18 that the people will *see* the difference. There is always a difference. God always makes a distinction between His children and those who persist in standing outside His family. But that difference is not always apparent; it cannot always be seen. In God's future, however, the distinction will be revealed in clearest terms. Those who serve God will fit one category, and those who do not will belong in another.

Behind the English phrase "treasured possession" lies a single Hebrew word that the prophet doubtless chose because of its special significance in Hebrew tradition. The word *segullah* means "a very special treasure" or "a highly valued property." Through the stories that relate the history of God's dealings with Israel, Israel is called God's *segullah*. So, for example, at the base of Mount Sinai, where Israel soon was to receive the commandments of God, a promise was made to the people of Israel: "Now if you obey me fully and keep my covenant, then out of all nations you will be my treasured possession" (Exod. 19:5). What a stunning thought! By faithfulness, by full obedience, by careful compliance with covenant requirements, the people of Israel could become known as God's favorite, the treasure that He prized above all other treasures. That this was not merely favoritism is clear from the rigid demands that are made of those who would claim such special status before God. And that this idea continued in force in subsequent eras may be learned by noting its reformulation throughout the Book of Deuteronomy (e.g., 7:6; 14:2; 26:18). Then in the New Testament a similar idea is reflected in Titus 2:14. There the self-sacrifice of Jesus is said to be for the ultimate purpose of creating a people who are so redeemed *from* wickedness and so purified *for* service to God that they become "his very own," His unique treasure, or as Malachi has stated it, His "treasured possession." Again, in Titus also it should be noted that those who desire such special status must say no to "ungodliness and worldly passions," as well as yes to "self-controlled, upright and godly lives" (2:12). And notice further that Titus also proclaims a lifestyle of hope. The people described above both negatively (opposed to sin) and positively (given to righteousness) must "wait for the blessed hope" (2:13) even when it cannot be seen! Could the author of Titus have been reading Malachi?

D. God's Day (4:1–3)

In the closing paragraph of his sermon, Malachi introduces two new figures of speech by which he explains the activity of God. There will be, as he has argued already, a "day" of God, a day on which He will right all wrongs and clear up all outstanding debts on His record book. That day will be perceived in two ways, depending on the character of the person involved. For some it will be viewed as a day of destruction. For these persons God's day will come as a burning furnace, destroying everyone guilty of arrogance in evildoing. They will flare into flame as quickly as does dry and highly combustible chaff (NIV "stubble"). Nothing will be left of them. No hope will exist for them. No future. No brighter day. All will be over, consumed in the mighty fire of God.

But that same day will afford healing warmth to other persons. Those who revered (feared, respected) God, whose lives had been adapted to a style of hope, who had lived in the present with an eye to the future, will be healed rather than consumed. The sun is certainly as hot as any furnace is; yet the sun's heat will bring healing, and its effect will extend to the most mundane areas of life.

These two figures (sun and furnace) prepare the way for Malachi's conclusion to this sermon. The righteous will cavort about with joy. The wicked will be trampled under their feet. Things will finally be right. Doubts will finally be laid to rest. God's fairness will finally be demonstrated beyond all question. And it will all occur, God says, "on the day when I *act*" (NIV "do these things") (v. 3). God is not out of control now, in the present. Things are not beyond His capability to cope. Life is not running wild. He is simply waiting for His moment, His day. Then He will act. And His action will be enough.

But once again the prophet is speaking in promissory fashion. As far as his audience could "see," nothing had changed. Right was still on the scaffold, and wrong still appeared to be on the throne. And the prophet does not, *cannot* point to the present with a new interpretation, a more positive evaluation of the situation. Instead, he calls thricefold for a lifestyle of hope, of a futuristic attitude for the believer. He calls for the people of God to believe that their God is still in charge even when the evidence is not all in. He refers, poetically, to God's book, but he really means to call for faith in God's character. If God is not going to bring true justice out of the present disorder of things, it really is futile to serve Him. And there the matter must stay. No one can *know* by observing circumstances. But a choice must still be made—to serve God or not. To respond in faithfulness to the future or to yield in weakness to the moment. To join the majority who prosper now or to wait in confidence with the minority who hope (with assurance) to become known as God's treasured possession.

Thus, complaining, harsh words are no longer necessary. The issue cannot be determined for the moment. But in the meantime:

Do you not know?
    Have you not heard?
The LORD is the everlasting God,
    the Creator of the ends of the earth.
He will not grow tired or weary,
    and his understanding no one can fathom.
He gives strength to the weary
    and increases the power of the weak.
Even youths grow tired and weary,
    and young men stumble and fall;
but those who *hope!* [!] in the LORD
    will renew their strength.
They will soar on wings like eagles;
    they will run and not grow weary,
    they will walk and not be faint.
                        (Isa. 40:28–31)

For Further Study

1. Do you believe it is "wrong" to question God? Could there ever be a time when harsh words would be an appropriate action to take with God?

2. Malachi preached two different sermons about the justice of God, this one and the one studied earlier in chapter 6. Which of the two do you think he would choose to preach to the congregation of which you are a member? Which one addresses your own personal situation more directly?

3. Do you believe that God really plans to "even the score" at some point in the future? Why do you think He does not act right now to end all injustice and to punish all evildoers? What would you do differently if you were God?

4. What are the advantages of a lifestyle featuring belief that is oriented toward the future? Are there any disadvantages?

5. Do you consider yourself to be a member of God's "special treasure"? Why or why not?

Chapter 9

The Conclusion
(Malachi 4:4–6)

It is generally acknowledged that these final three verses are an editorial addition to the Book of Malachi. It is apparent that they do not share the structural characteristics of the six major sermons that comprise the heart of the book. Nor do they participate in a meaningful way in the messages of the major sermons. In fact, some scholars have supposed that these final verses were added to serve as an appendix to the entire body of the twelve "Minor Prophets."

Nevertheless, there are some significant assertions made in this final paragraph that warrant attention. The first of these pertains to the Mosaic law, mentioned in verse 4. The word *remember* in a context like this means far more than merely to think about something in the past. This word carries the idea of re-creation, reidentification with the past, even a reexperiencing of important moments of faith. Thus, to remember the teachings of Moses would be to bring them out of the past and into the present, to invest them with current meaning and authority, to begin anew to order life on the basis of their point of view. Further, the English word *law* is a very poor substitute for the Hebrew word *torah*. *Torah* was not merely legal statutes (dos and don'ts) and lifeless rules and regulations; it was rather instruction, teaching, and example. In Israelite usage *torah* came to stand for divine revelation in much the same way described earlier for *davar* and *massa'*, used in Malachi 1:1. Thus, a rereading of the entire series of sermons of Malachi would show that basic to the spiritual problem of Israel was their tendency to forget the past, to forget the teachings of God through Moses by which their life as a nation had been so well ordered in earlier years. Malachi 4:4 is an attempt to correct that problem by calling for a return to those basic tenets of faith and practice. Indeed, if the call for a return to God in 3:7 were to be taken seriously, what other starting place could there be but the Mosaic teachings?

A second assertion is related to the identification of Elijah as the messenger of the Lord who would return to Israel before the "great and dreadful day of the Lord" (4:5). But this identification alters the function of the messenger (introduced in 3:1) to what is basically a social task—the turning of hearts in an attempt to restore the family harmony that had been disrupted by divorce and mixed marriages (see 2:10-16). So important was this Elijan function perceived to be that Jewish tradition stipulated that whenever the Book of Malachi was read in the synagogue, the fifth verse must be repeated after the sixth verse was read. In this way the book can be made to end on a positive rather than on a negative note. In short, the work of Elijah was to be a powerful social influence much to be desired.

The final assertion in the Conclusion is related to the decision of the editor to end the canonical form of the book with the word *curse*. Unless, it was asserted, the reforming measures of Elijah were brought about, God would come to smite the country with such a bane. The word *curse* here does not mean quite the same thing as that described in earlier verses (1:14; 3:9). The Hebrew word here *(herem)* is different from the word used earlier, and the concept it represents is different. A *herem* means a thing devoted totally to and set aside for destruction. The people against whom Israel had fought in earlier years had been set aside for this kind of destruction (e.g., see Josh. 6:17). But never had Israel been set aside to be destroyed. Such a prospect was indeed frightening, and it was a fate to be avoided at any cost.

For Further Study

1. Read articles on the law *(torah)*, Moses, and Elijah in a Bible dictionary or an encyclopedia listed in the bibliography. What links these three together?

2. What are the significant elements of the Christian faith that need to be remembered in a systematic fashion?

3. The celebration of the Lord's Supper is known as something done "in *remembrance* of" Jesus. What is the meaning of the word *remembrance* in this phrase?

4. List several topics or subjects on which you have heard a sermon preached recently. Would Malachi have anything important to say about any of these?

Bibliography

Commentaries on Malachi

Dentan, R. C. "The Book of Malachi," *Interpreter's Bible*, vol. 6. New York/ Nashville: Abingdon, 1956.

Edgar, S. L. *The Minor Prophets [Excluding Amos, Hosea and Micah]*. London: Epworth, 1962.

Hailey, Homer. *A Commentary on the Minor Prophets*. Grand Rapids: Baker, 1972.

Mason, Rex. *The Books of Haggai, Zechariah and Malachi, Cambridge Bible Commentary*. Cambridge University Press, 1978.

Paterson, John. *The Goodly Fellowship of the Prophets*. New York: Scribner, 1948.

Smith, George Adam. *The Twelve Minor Prophets*. Vol. 2: *The Expositor's Bible*. New York: Doran, 1928.

Smith, J. M. Powis. "A Critical and Exegetical Commentary on the Book of Malachi," *The International Critical Commentary*. New York: Scribner, 1912.

Wolf, Herbert. *Haggai and Malachi: Rededication and Renewal*. Chicago: Moody, 1976.

Bible Dictionaries and Encyclopedias

Buttrick, George Arthur, ed. *The Interpreter's Dictionary of the Bible*. 4 vols. New York/Nashville: Abingdon, 1962. A *Supplementary* volume is now available from the same publisher.

Douglas, J. D., ed. *The New Bible Dictionary*. Grand Rapids: Eerdmans, 1970.

Tenney, Merrill C., ed. *The Zondervan Pictorial Bible Dictionary*. rev. ed. Grand Rapids: Zondervan, 1967.

————. *The Zondervan Pictorial Encyclopedia of the Bible*. 5 vols. Grand Rapids: Zondervan, 1975.

Bible Translations

Jerusalem Bible
New American Standard Bible
New English Bible
New International Version
Revised Standard Version

Special Studies

Anderson, Bernhard W. "Exodus Typology in Second Isaiah." In *Israel's Prophetic Heritage.* Edited by Bernhard W. Anderson and Walter Harrelson. New York: Harper and Row, 1962, pp. 177-96.

Bright, John. *Covenant and Promise.* Philadelphia: Westminster, 1976. Read especially the final two chapters, which discuss the issue of future hope in ancient Israel from the time of Jeremiah and later.

Brueggemann, Walter. *The Prophetic Imagination.* Philadelphia: Fortress, 1978.

Sanders, James A. *Torah and Canon.* Philadelphia: Fortress, 1972. This is the classic statement about ways in which the canon of Scripture grew to become authoritative in the life of the people of God.

Tucker, Gene. "Prophetic Superscriptions and the Growth of a Canon." In *Canon and Authority.* Edited by George W. Coats and Burke O. Long. Philadelphia: Fortress, 1977, pp. 56-70.